From Burnout to Bliss

From Burnout to Bliss

Fall Back in Love with Teaching

Kimberly G. McDowell

BLOOMSBURY ACADEMIC
NEW YORK • LONDON • OXFORD • NEW DELHI • SYDNEY

BLOOMSBURY ACADEMIC
Bloomsbury Publishing Inc, 1359 Broadway, New York, NY 10018, USA
Bloomsbury Publishing Plc, 50 Bedford Square, London, WC1B 3DP, UK
Bloomsbury Publishing Ireland, 29 Earlsfort Terrace, Dublin 2, D02 AY28, Ireland

BLOOMSBURY, BLOOMSBURY ACADEMIC and the Diana logo are trademarks of Bloomsbury Publishing Plc

First published in the United States of America 2026

A catalog record for this book is available from the Library of Congress

ISBN: HB: 979-8-7651-8894-1
PB: 979-8-7651-8895-8
ePDF: 979-8-216-35183-2
eBook: 979-8-7651-8896-5

Typeset by Integra Software Services Pvt. Ltd.

For product safety related questions contact productsafety@bloomsbury.com.

To find out more about our authors and books visit www.bloomsbury.com and sign up for our newsletters.

To each and every student I have had in my classroom.
Thank you for teaching me more than I thought I could learn.

Contents

Introduction

I love schools. I love teaching.

I remember playing school on the back porch with my best friend Heidi. We always argued about who would be the teacher—she usually won, so we did a lot of spelling tests, but it was still fun.

I love numbers. I love math.

When I was little, I named my kitten Eighty-Six. I also told my mom that my peas tasted like a straight line. Numbers, shapes, and patterns give me comfort. They make sense, and they are beautiful.

So, it came as no surprise to anyone when I chose to become a math teacher. Over the years, I've taught in a variety of settings, from high schools to colleges. While I've enjoyed every experience, I've discovered that my heart beats a little faster in high schools—there's just something special about that environment that draws me in.

Believe me, I'm fully aware of how lucky I am to fall in love with something and then get to do it for over thirty-five years—and counting. It's a gift, like finding a rare baseball card or a Wi-Fi connection that consistently works. It's both an honor and a privilege, and honestly, I can't wait to jump out of bed each morning to do the work (though, let's be real, I might hit the snooze button once or twice). But once I'm up, it's all enthusiasm and passion. I mean, who wouldn't be excited to spend their days doing something they truly love? It's not just a job; it's a lifelong adventure—and I'm here for every minute of it.

I also know many people do not share my passion for mathematics. When I am at a party and mention I teach AP Calculus, people usually cringe, tell me how much they hate math, and take a step away from me. Some even ask me how I can spend so much time with teenagers. Nonetheless, I am proud to be a high school math teacher, and I want more people to realize teaching is a fun, rewarding, challenging, exhausting, fulfilling, hard, all-consuming, satisfying, diverse, and a great job, let alone a great way to live your life. But even I must admit, something has been lost along the way.

If you're a teacher, you know this struggle intimately. Disheartening experiences can lead to fatigue, anxiety, and depression. Left unmanaged, this can turn into burnout and the desire to quit teaching.

Each day, responsibilities multiply while the things you hope to let go of linger like shadows, and the weight of expectations can feel like an anchor. Nothing is being taken off your plate. You are often put into situations you are not prepared for. You might find yourself questioning whether your efforts truly matter, wondering if the long hours and heartfelt dedication are making any real impact at all. But let me reassure you—*they absolutely do*. Even on days when appreciation feels like a distant memory and support seems elusive, *know that you are valued*. When you doubt whether anyone notices your hard work, remember this: *they do*. Your influence reaches far beyond the classroom, shaping lives and inspiring futures in ways you may never fully realize. Trust me, this is true.

My friend, if you're feeling burnt out or on the brink of it, I am truly sorry. This book is here for you. It will invite you, if you are ready, to reclaim the joy in your work through insightful questions, a focus on gratitude, a fresh perspective, and a sprinkle of humor. A happy and healthy you doesn't just enhance your own life; it also enriches the learning experiences of your students. Go back and read that sentence again. Isn't that what we, as teachers, aspire to achieve? *Your happiness is good for everyone. It is not a selfish endeavor. It is necessary for you to be the teacher you want to be.*

Let's embark on an inspiring journey filled with renewed enthusiasm and purpose. Give yourself permission to focus on yourself. After all, you are the only person you can truly change. Together, we'll share laughter and tears, delve deep, and rediscover our passions. These insights will empower us to support ourselves, our students, and our colleagues. Are you ready to discover just how extraordinary you truly are as an educator? Are you ready to reclaim your best self?

Part 1
The *Big Picture* Questions

A Quick Note to New Teachers

Dear Amazing New Teacher,

If you are preparing to enter the classroom or are already in the early years of your teaching journey, I want to begin with this simple, heartfelt message: **thank you.**

Thank you for choosing this path—a path that is as demanding as it is rewarding, as humbling as it is profound. Thank you for bringing your time, your talents, your energy, and your heart to a profession that has the power to change lives. Thank you for standing up each day for students who need what only you can offer: your patience, your creativity, your wisdom, your love, your kindness, and your belief in their potential.

You have chosen a life of service, and that choice matters. It matters to your students, to your colleagues, to your community, to the future you are helping shape, and it matters to you. Teaching is not simply a job—it's a calling. It calls for compassion, resilience, flexibility, and an unwavering commitment to growth—not only the growth of your students, but your own.

The second thing I want to offer you is a gentle reminder: burnout does not have to be part of your story. I sincerely hope it never will be. But if you ever feel the weight of this work press too heavily on your shoulders—if the joy begins to dim or the days feel longer than they should—I hope you'll reach for this book. Keep it nearby. Let it remind you that you are not alone. Let it offer you practical strategies and quiet encouragement. Let it help you avoid the pitfalls that so many of us have stumbled into.

The reflections and lessons in these pages are drawn from research, conversations with educators, and years of personal experience—through triumphs and missteps, moments of doubt, and times of deep fulfillment. I don't claim to have all the answers, and this book won't eliminate every challenging day or difficult season. But what I can offer is perspective, hard-earned insight, and a steadfast belief in your ability to thrive.

Please, remember to care for yourself with the same compassion you extend so generously to your students. Stay connected—to your colleagues, your mentors, your community, and to the deeper "why" that brought you here in the first place. Hold on to the joy, even on the hard days.

As teachers, it's important to pause and remember just how profoundly fortunate we are. Every day, parents, guardians, administrators, and entire communities place their trust in us to nurture and guide what they value most—their children, their future. This is no small responsibility. We are entrusted not only with educating minds but also with shaping character, inspiring growth, and fostering potential in students of all ages. It is both a profound responsibility and a deep honor to serve in this role. Amid the challenges, may we never lose sight of the incredible privilege it is to be a part of our students' journeys. We are so lucky!

So, embrace laughter—frequently and freely. Take time to honor the small wins, the quiet triumphs that might otherwise go unnoticed. Discover joy in the chaos, wonder in the creativity, and meaning in the beautifully unpredictable rhythm of each day. Teaching is not just a profession; it's an evolving art form—a daily practice of empathy, ingenuity, and intentional care. It's about forging connections, offering guidance, and fostering growth—not only in your students, but within yourself as well. Each moment in the classroom is an opportunity to learn, to adapt, and to inspire.

And once again, from the bottom of my heart: **thank you for choosing to teach.** May this journey bring you purpose, growth, and joy. I hope you will look back on your choice to teach, years from now, with pride, no regrets, and the knowledge that you have made the world a better place.

With my sincerest gratitude and encouragement,
kim

How Do You Read This Book?

You don't have to read this book in any particular order. In fact, the chapters were intentionally arranged without a strict sequence. Flip back to the Table of Contents and see what catches your eye. If your curiosity is *piqued*, start there. If nothing stands out, simply dive in anywhere—but be prepared to answer some deeply personal questions.

This book is built around questions. Part I tackles the big-picture issues of teaching and teacher burnout. Part II zooms in on the everyday realities of life in a school. Each chapter begins with a question designed to help you reflect and uncover your own insights.

Once you've read as much as you like (and I hope you'll come back to revisit some chapters), I'd love to hear your thoughts. My email is kmcdowell256@gmail.com. Let me know if anything resonated with you. I would also love to know if you were looking for a chapter that wasn't there. Maybe we can work on it together in the next book.

Enjoy and happy teaching!

1 *Why Are Teachers So Special?*

Teachers are some of the most incredible and underrated people on the planet. I'll never forget when my son first started reading. His teacher played a pivotal role in his growth, and I couldn't help but feel an overwhelming sense of love and gratitude for her. She gave him what we, as parents, struggled to provide. (Thank you, Chrissy!) She was the one who helped him unlock the world of reading in a way that was meaningful and lasting. To have such a direct and positive influence on a child's life is something truly special. She wasn't just a teacher—she was a guiding force, and I will always be thankful for the difference she made in my son's and my family's lives.

In my own journey, there have been many guiding forces—teachers who gave me something invaluable that I could never repay. A math teacher who made learning fun and exciting, a college professor who believed in me and pushed me to apply for a prestigious fellowship, and a coach who taught me the value of hard work and perseverance. These mentors helped shape who I am, and their influence stays with me every day.

I'm sure you, too, have had teachers who did more than just follow the job description. Maybe you had a teacher who saw you when no one else did, who believed in you when you couldn't believe in yourself, or who challenged you to rise higher than you thought you could. It's likely these teachers are the reason you chose to become one yourself. They're the ones who inspired you to give back—to become the kind of teacher who empowers and inspires the next generation.

Here is a wonderful story about an elementary school teacher who represents what all of this means:

Her name was Mrs. Thompson. And as she stood in front of her 5th grade class on the very first day of school, she told the children a lie. Like most teachers, she looked at her students and said that she loved them all the same. But that was impossible, because there in the front row, slumped in his seat, was a little boy named Teddy Stoddard. Mrs. Thompson had watched Teddy the year before and noticed that he didn't play well with the other children, that his clothes were messy and that he constantly needed a bath. And Teddy could be unpleasant. It got to the point where Mrs. Thompson would take delight in marking his papers with a broad red pen, making bold X's and then putting a big "F" at the top of his papers.

At the school where Mrs. Thompson taught, she was required to review each child's past records and she put Teddy's off until last. However, when she reviewed his file, she was in for a surprise. Teddy's first grade teacher wrote, "Teddy is a bright child with a ready laugh. He does his work neatly and has good manners … he is a joy to be around." His second-grade teacher wrote, "Teddy is an excellent student, well-liked by his classmates, but he is troubled because his mother has a terminal illness and life at home must be a struggle." His third-grade teacher wrote, "His mother's death has been hard on him. He tries to do his best, but his father doesn't show much interest, and his home life will soon affect him if some steps aren't taken."

Teddy's fourth grade teacher wrote, "Teddy is withdrawn and doesn't show much interest in school. He doesn't have many friends and sometimes sleeps in class." By now, Mrs. Thompson realized the problem and she was ashamed of herself. She felt even worse when her students brought her Christmas presents, wrapped in beautiful ribbons and bright paper, except for Teddy's. His present was clumsily wrapped in the heavy, brown paper that he got from a grocery store. Mrs. Thompson took pains to open it in the middle of the other presents. Some of the children started to laugh when she found a rhinestone bracelet with some of the stones missing and a bottle that was one-quarter full of perfume. But she stifled the children's laughter when she exclaimed how pretty the bracelet was, putting it on, and dabbing some of the perfume on her wrist.

Teddy Stoddard stayed after school that day just long enough to say, "Mrs. Thompson, today you smelled just like my mom used to." After the children left, she cried for at least an hour. On that very day, she quit teaching reading, and writing, and arithmetic. Instead, she began to teach children. Mrs. Thompson paid particular attention to Teddy. As she worked with him, his mind seemed to come alive. The more she encouraged him, the faster he responded. By the end of the year, Teddy had become one of the smartest children in the class and, despite her lie that she would love all the children the same, Teddy became one of her "teacher's pets."

A year later, she found a note under her door, from Teddy, telling her that she was still the best teacher he ever had in his whole life. Six years went by before she got another note from Teddy. He then wrote that he had finished high school, third in his class, and she was still the best teacher he ever had in his whole life. Four years after that, she got another letter, saying that while things had been tough at times, he'd stayed in school, had stuck with it, and would soon graduate from college with the highest of honors. He assured Mrs. Thompson that she was still the best and favorite teacher he ever had in his whole life.

Then four more years passed and yet another letter came. This time he explained that after he got his bachelor's degree, he decided to go a little further. The letter explained that she was still the best and favorite teacher he ever had. But now his name was a little longer. The letter was signed, Theodore F. Stoddard, MD. The story doesn't end there. You see, there was yet another letter that spring. Teddy said he'd met this girl and was going to be married. He explained that his father had died a couple of years ago and he was wondering if Mrs. Thompson might agree to sit in the place at the wedding that was usually reserved for the mother of the groom.

Of course, Mrs. Thompson did. And guess what? She wore that bracelet, the one with several rhinestones missing. And she made sure she was wearing the perfume that Teddy remembered his mother wearing on their last Christmas together. They hugged each other, and Dr. Stoddard whispered in Mrs. Thompson's ear, "Thank you, Mrs. Thompson, for believing in me. Thank you so much for making me feel important and showing me that I could make a difference." Mrs. Thompson, with tears in her eyes, whispered back. She said, "Teddy, you have it all wrong. You were the one who taught me that I could make a difference. I didn't know how to teach until I met you."[1]

Why do these incredible individuals—our teachers—so often receive such a bad rap? If you only read the headlines in our country, you might think that our education system is on the brink of collapse and that teachers are failing in their roles. But I'm here to tell you that nothing could be further from the truth.

In a recent survey published in *The Educator*, 84 percent of the 996 respondents said they had "more good teachers than bad teachers."[2] Yet, the same survey revealed that over 61 percent of people never told their favorite teacher how much they meant to them.[3] This gap in recognition suggests that teachers are not always shown the appreciation they deserve.

A key issue that defines teachers is standardized testing, yet these test scores fail to capture the full scope of a teacher's impact. Teachers are not just educators—they are mentors, guides, and sources of inspiration. Much of this crucial work happens beyond the walls of the classroom. In fact, over 54 percent of survey respondents shared that their favorite teacher made a lasting impression by offering support outside of regular school hours.[4]

It's clear: teachers are doing more than many realize, and they are rarely shown the gratitude they deserve. So, the question is—Can we change this? Can we make sure our teachers know just how much they are loved and valued? This might be one of the keys to addressing teacher burnout.

2 *What Is Teacher Burnout?*

Did you know that teachers are evenly split over whether they would advise a young person starting out today to become a teacher? Only 48 percent say they would, and 52 percent say they would not. Among those who've been teaching for less than six years, 57 percent say they'd recommend teaching as a career. That number drops sharply to just 45 percent among teachers with more than a decade of experience.[1]

A major reason for this is teacher burnout. What is teacher burnout? If you're an educator, you already know the answer all too well. Teacher burnout is the overwhelming weight of responsibilities that makes your job harder than it should be. It's the exhaustion that comes from constantly giving your time, energy, and heart without enough recognition or support.

Teacher burnout is feeling invisible—when no one acknowledges the effort you put in every minute of every day. It's carrying the emotional and academic needs of your students while navigating endless meetings, changing policies, and unrealistic expectations. It's the frustration of wanting to do what's best for your students but lacking the time, support, resources, or energy to make it happen. Teacher burnout is when the thought of walking through the school's doors fills you with dread and you don't know how you will make it through the day.

Most of all, teacher burnout is the creeping feeling of depletion—the sense that you have nothing left to give. It's the loss of joy in a profession you once loved, replaced by fatigue, frustration, and the thought that maybe, just maybe, you can't keep going like this.

But here's the thing: burnout isn't a personal failure. It's a symptom of a broken system that asks too much and gives too little in return. Recognizing it is the first step toward reclaiming your passion and finding ways to fall back in love with teaching.

Let's take a closer look. Teacher burnout is a significant and often unspoken challenge that affects educators at all stages of their careers, regardless of age or gender. Burnout is the leading cause of teachers leaving the profession, underscoring the pervasive nature of this issue. By addressing burnout and helping educators rediscover their passion for teaching, we can improve teacher retention and tackle the shortage of educators in our country. Ultimately, this will lead to a better educational experience for our students. More importantly, addressing your burnout is important. Let's name it, accept it, and then start to make your job better.

So, what exactly is burnout? The World Health Organization (WHO) defines burnout as "a syndrome conceptualized as resulting from chronic workplace stress that has not been successfully managed. It is characterized by three dimensions: feelings of energy depletion or exhaustion; increased mental distance from one's job, or feelings of negativism or cynicism related to one's job; and reduced professional efficacy."[2] In *Psychology Today*, burnout was described as "a state of chronic stress that leads to physical and emotional exhaustion, cynicism, detachment and feelings of ineffectiveness and lack of accomplishment."[3] Can you relate to this? Most teachers can.

According to the National Education Association, teacher burnout can be defined as "a condition in which an educator has exhausted the personal and professional resources necessary to do the job."[4] That is a sobering definition. One you can no doubt relate to. Some of you might even be thinking, what resources?

Herbert Freudenberger coined the term *burnout* in 1970.[5] He said that professions that involve a strong sense of morality or purpose and commitment from workers who sacrifice themselves for the good of others were most at risk.[6] In addition to this, teachers are usually high achievers who like to work hard for their students and are always looking for ways to improve. This makes teaching the perfect storm for high levels of burnout, and we can see this in the data. The US Bureau of Labor Statistics (BLS) reported that 270,000 teachers have left teaching each year since 2016 and projects this rate of departure to continue through 2026.[7]

In 2024, Pew Research Center reported that 84 percent of teachers don't have enough time to do their work, and it is only getting worse.[8] Student needs are increasing, parents' demands are growing, and dictates on teachers' time are multiplying.[9] Teachers are asked to do more and more. No wonder we are stressed. No wonder we are burnt out. This book will not ask you to do more. In fact, it will ask that you do less, but we will get to that later. How can you do what you already do differently?

Let's take one last look at the numbers. A survey conducted in 2023 said that 78 percent of teachers said they were stressed, 89 percent of teachers experienced symptoms of poor mental health due to their work, and 55 percent of teachers said their school's culture has a negative effect on their well-being.[10] It's that last statistic that we are going to focus on here—school culture. I strongly believe that we can tackle burnout by focusing on yourself and your school's culture. Are you ready to take back your job?

3 What Is Teacher Retention?

Teacher retention is an important issue that can be understood in two key ways. First, it refers to a school's ability to reduce teacher turnover. What strategies does your school have in place to support and retain its educators? Second, teacher retention has emerged as a complex field of study that examines the factors influencing teachers' decisions to stay at or leave their positions. The research on this topic is both insightful and compelling. Why do teachers stay? Why do teachers leave?

The Learning Policy Institute, in its article *Teacher Turnover: Why It Matters and What We Can Do About It*, highlights a troubling trend in US education:

> *While shortages tend to draw attention to recruitment, this report finds that 90% of open teaching positions are created by teachers who leave the profession. While some leave due to retirement, about two-thirds of teachers depart for other reasons, most often due to dissatisfaction with their work. Teacher attrition in the United States is roughly twice as high as in high-performing regions such as Finland, Singapore, and Ontario, Canada.*[1]

This raises an important question: Why is teacher turnover so much higher in the United States compared to other high-achieving countries?

As thought-provoking as this question is, let's focus on a more personal question for a moment: What do you think your school is doing to keep you as a teacher? If your immediate response is "nothing," let's acknowledge that feeling and admit that it can be discouraging. There are likely two possibilities here. First, you might be absolutely right: your school may not truly value its teachers. Or, second, your school may value you, but you just aren't seeing it. Which of these feels more accurate to you?

Would you be open to trying something? I recommend taking a moment to focus on the positive aspects of your school—those things that highlight how you, along with the faculty and staff, are truly valued. Try looking for things that you are thankful for. These may be big or small, but they matter. For instance, do you have access to good healthcare? Does the school offer a retirement savings plan? Is there a wellness program or other resources to support your well-being? Are there simple comforts like a coffee machine, a faculty lounge, or even a decent parking spot and bathroom? Do your colleagues support you and know you as a person? What are the things, both large and small, that make your job easier or more fulfilling?

Here's something interesting: When you start asking yourself, "What am I thankful for?" it can help shift your perspective. By focusing on the positive aspects of your job—even the small ones—they begin to accumulate, and your overall view of your work can improve. Sometimes, simply noticing the good things around you can make your entire environment feel brighter.

Now, this doesn't mean the challenges disappear. I'm not suggesting that at all. What I am suggesting is that when you intentionally look for the positives, you'll start to notice them more. It's like learning a new word—you start hearing it everywhere once you become aware of the word and its meaning.

Let's tie this back to teacher retention. Do you think some of the positives you see in your environment are intentional? Could your school be deliberately creating these positive experiences to help keep you happy and engaged? The answer might be no, but it's worth considering.

Here's another question: If you were in charge, what would you do to support teachers and keep them at your school? Are any of your ideas already being put into practice? Does what you see suggest that teacher retention is a priority for your school? Exploring these questions could offer valuable insights into what is already being done that you haven't noticed before. You may have people at your school who are working hard, and not many people are seeing or appreciating what they are doing. Sound familiar?

You should not take it upon yourself to make your school a place where teachers want to come back year after year. If you have some good ideas, that is great. But be careful, we are focusing on you. Just the awareness that things are being done for you is enough right now. Sometimes, trying to implement change can be frustrating if no one is listening to you.

What have we learned from the work that is being done around teacher retention? The research shows that K-12 teachers are among the most burnt-out professionals in the United States. Over 44 percent of teachers report feeling "often or always" burnt out, and more than half of US teachers are planning to leave the profession earlier than they originally intended.[2] The top reasons for this burnout include lack of compensation, excessive expectations, well-being concerns, leadership issues, and limited workplace flexibility.

On the flip side, why do teachers stay in the profession? According to recent research, 58 percent of teachers stay because of the meaningful work they do. Other important factors include supportive coworkers (39 percent), compensation (34 percent), geography (28 percent), and a sense of community (27 percent).[3]

Of the five key reasons for staying in teaching, three revolve around people: our students, our colleagues, and the broader community. While much attention is given to the financial investment in schools, less is said about the emotional investment. The investment schools put into their faculty and staff. In his book *Unreasonable Hospitality*, Will Guidara reflects on a concept his friend Danny Meyer calls "Enlightened Hospitality."[4] This idea challenges traditional hierarchies by prioritizing the well-being of employees above all else—even above that of guests or investors. While Will and Danny's work was rooted in the restaurant industry, their insights into understanding and supporting people are universally applicable, offering valuable lessons for any field, including education.

Let me be clear: I'm not suggesting that teachers should be valued more than students. What I'm advocating for is that if administrators and school boards prioritized the well-being of teachers, students would ultimately benefit from having happier, more productive, and more engaged educators. Perhaps this is the first step in improving teacher retention.

In addition to prioritizing the well-being of teachers, administrators must also cultivate a culture of trust. When teachers feel trusted to do their jobs and are given the autonomy to excel, it has a profound impact on their job satisfaction and retention. Research consistently shows that trust is a crucial factor in why teachers remain in the profession. However, for this trust to be effective, accountability must also be in place to ensure success for both educators and the broader school community. We will explore the role of accountability in more detail in a later chapter.

4 *What Is Teaching?*

This Is an Intriguing Question: What Is Teaching?

Remember, we are tackling the big questions first. Many teachers would offer a variety of definitions so, who is right? Ultimately, each teacher's definition is valid, as it reflects their own unique perspective and experience with the art of teaching. The other cool thing about this question is that the way you answer this dictates how you teach.

There is a lot that has been written about *how* to teach and *what* to teach. With new research on the value of sleep for adolescents (and everyone), there has even been a lot said about *when* to teach but the *who* of teaching has not been looked at as closely.

In his famous quote, Hiam Ginott said,

> *I've come to a frightening conclusion that I am the decisive element in the classroom. It's my personal approach that creates the climate. It's my daily mood that makes the weather. As a teacher, I possess a tremendous power to make a child's life miserable or joyous. I can be a tool of torture or an instrument of inspiration. I can humiliate or heal. In all situations, it is my response that decides whether a crisis will be escalated or de-escalated and a child humanized or dehumanized.*[1]

As you can see, who you are as a teacher matters considerably.

Recognizing the pivotal role of the teacher, any definition of teaching should encompass the teacher's core and authentic self. It's easy to overlook this when we focus too much on pedagogically sound definitions, missing the bigger picture. But it's crucial to remember: who you are is the most important element in your teaching. To teach effectively, you must first know yourself—understand who you are and why you teach. Ensure that your teaching comes from your authentic self.

One of the most valuable pieces of advice you can follow is this: teach through the lens of your true self. Authenticity is powerful, and your students can sense when it's missing. They don't need a performance—they need a real, engaged educator who connects with them in a genuine way. If you find yourself adopting a persona every time you step in front of the class, take a moment to reflect. Ask yourself why. Is it out of habit, expectation, or fear of showing vulnerability? Teaching isn't about playing a role; it's about being fully present and open. When you embrace your true self, you create a space where students feel safe to do the same. That kind of authenticity fosters trust, deeper learning, and meaningful relationships—gifts that will serve both you and your students well beyond the classroom.

In addition to being authentic, one of the most important insights in education is understanding that teaching and learning are not the same. Just because something is taught does not mean it has been learned. Many teachers mistakenly assume that delivering a lesson guarantees comprehension, but effective educators recognize this gap and work diligently to bridge it.

This is where assessments become invaluable. They serve not only as tools for measuring student progress but also as critical feedback for the teacher, revealing whether instruction has successfully translated into understanding. Thoughtfully designed assessments help identify misconceptions, guide instructional adjustments, and ensure that students are truly grasping the material.

Recognizing this distinction between teaching and learning is essential when evaluating a lesson or grading an assessment. It shifts the focus from merely covering content to fostering deep comprehension. After all, the best teachers are lifelong learners themselves—constantly reflecting, adapting, and growing alongside their students.

So, one definition of teaching is showing up as your true self, rolling up your sleeves and sharing, learning, and growing with the students in your room. What is your definition of teaching?

In the end, teaching is not just about delivering content but about showing up as your authentic self. It's about building meaningful connections with your students, fostering trust and respect, and creating an environment where both teaching and learning thrive. By recognizing the distinction between teaching and learning, you're better equipped to reflect, adapt, and grow alongside your students. So, as you move forward, ask yourself: What is teaching to *you?* How will your answer help you be the best version of yourself?

5 *Why Do You Teach?*

Another Big Question

Some teachers teach because they are passionate about inspiring students and helping them realize that they can achieve anything they set their hearts to. They find joy in engaging with students, guiding their ideas, and fostering an environment of growth, curiosity, kindness, and open-mindedness. They believe it's essential to show students that they are heard, valued, cared for, and loved. Teaching is not just about academics—it's about nurturing the whole person. To do this, you must let go of yourself and invest in them. Letting go of yourself and serving others is truly a gift, and a life of service is one of the most fulfilling and meaningful lives one can lead.

Many teachers love teaching because they love the fact that each day is different from the last or the next. Someone said that the definition of despair is believing nothing will change. Well, spend time in a school—everything changes all the time. It could be the daily schedule that is always different, the athletic season, the mood of the classroom, the curriculum, the dress code, or the attendance policy. Change is good, but you need to be flexible and a team player to enjoy the ride.

Teaching is not sitting at a desk with earbuds in and getting your work done. Teaching is serving others. This basic tenet of teaching has been lost along the way. Teachers need to realize that they are the servants to our youth. Now, this does not mean that we work for them or honor their every whim. Of course not. It means, when we walk into the room, our goal is their growth. Their needs demand our attention. They are the focus of our time and energy.

Unfortunately, our society doesn't always recognize or honor the importance of serving others as it should. As a teacher, you may already feel underappreciated or underpaid, but it's crucial to leave those emotions behind when you step into your classroom. Your students are not responsible for the challenges you face, and you need to make peace with this, or else you are not serving your students as well as you could.

Yes, there are some negatives to the job, but there are also many unseen or unrecognized positives. For example, as a high school teacher, I can pursue my passions in the form of a team or a club. If I love journalism, I can be the advisor for the school paper. If I love ice hockey, I can coach one of the teams. If I love knitting, I can teach students how to knit at lunch. The possibilities are endless. You can travel the world, explore local politics, sponsor an internship with your favorite restaurant. See? Teaching is a great job!

So, why do you teach? Keep in mind that what brought you into teaching may not be what keeps you teaching.

Jamie Escalante, an educational hero, was a mathematics teacher at Garfield High School in East Los Angeles, California. He taught because he believed in his students. As a mathematics teacher, "he was able to teach children who had nothing and who had been 'taught' they could do nothing that they were capable of great things. He showed the world that with a good teacher poor and minority children can accomplish wonders."[1]

Maria Montessori, a pioneer in early childhood education, devoted her life to promoting a child-centered approach that emphasized independence and self-discovery.[2] She tirelessly advanced the Montessori Method through extensive lectures, numerous publications, and the development of a comprehensive teacher training program. Her deep belief in this philosophy led her to establish her own school—an initiative that ultimately sparked an educational revolution. Even if one doesn't fully embrace her methods, the depth of her passion and unwavering commitment to children's growth and development is undeniable.

Bill Nye, *The Science Guy*, taught because he loved science and wanted to show students that science was accessible to everyone.[3] His approach emphasized fun, humor, and hands-on experience. If you ever saw one of his shows, you would have to admit, he was having fun, and so were the kids.

As mentioned earlier, the *why* behind your teaching is a crucial factor in shaping *how* you teach. It's important to take time to reflect on why you started teaching in the first place. If your answer doesn't align with your authentic self, it might be worth reconsidering your path.

Teaching is a deeply personal profession, and it requires you to bring your true self into the classroom every day. Without that connection, it can be difficult to fully engage or inspire others. So, let me ask again, why do you teach?

6 *What Does a Good Day Look Like?*

Let's look at one last big picture question. This one is important to keep in your mind as you read further. Since one of the goals of this book is bliss—or to help you experience more good days at work, it is important to know: What does a "good day" look like to you?

Imagine this: we're meeting for an early dinner at a fantastic restaurant. I arrive early and snag a great table. You walk in a few minutes late, apologizing, "Sorry I'm late, I had to finish up at work." I ask how your day went, and you flash a smile and say, "It was a good day."

At that moment, before we even order drinks or appetizers, I'm dying to know more. What made it such a good day? What happened that turned it into something worth smiling about?

These are the kinds of days we're striving for—but in order to create more of them, we first need to recognize what makes them good and even great. When we know what truly makes a day fulfilling, we can aim for it more consciously and consistently.

As you think about what makes a day good for you, I am going to suggest thinking about more than the obvious. When I say obvious, I mean students were engaged, the classroom was productive, students loved the lesson, and they loved learning. Even though those are all good reasons to have a good day, let's go beyond that. What are some more subtle aspects of your day that would help make it great?

Let me share a few of my own discoveries that help me make my days good. One of the biggest things I've learned is that I can't sit still for too long. In the classroom, I'm always moving, but during faculty meetings or other duties, I find myself sitting for extended periods. I've realized that getting up and walking around, even for just a few minutes, helps me stay energized and focused more than I expected. If I can't get up and walk around the room, I'll head to the bathroom or take a short stroll around the building—anything to reset and keep a positive outlook.

Another discovery is that I know I work best in the morning. So, I try to schedule my most challenging or demanding tasks during that time. It's not always possible, but when I can, tackling the "heavy lifting" in the early hours makes the rest of my day feel more manageable and productive.

Finally, I've learned to deal with my boredom—something I never thought I'd have to manage. It may sound odd, especially when we all have so much to do, but there are times when I just can't focus on my To-Do list and find myself with a bit of downtime. I've learned that sitting with colleagues who are complaining or simply sitting at my desk doing nothing is the quickest way to let boredom take over. So, I've found ways to use those moments productively. For example, twice a week in the afternoons, I volunteer in the school library, knowing that I'm available to help students if needed. And when boredom randomly strikes, I make a habit of visiting other teachers' classrooms to observe what they're doing. It's not only a great way to break the monotony, but it's also one of the best ways to improve as a teacher—something I highly recommend.

These small discoveries have had a profound impact on how I approach my day, helping me find more enjoyment and fulfillment. What about you? Here are some questions to reflect on:

- What part of the day is the most challenging for you?
- Are there tasks you truly dislike doing? Why?
- When do you feel frustrated, and what tends to trigger those feelings?
- Who do you enjoy being around to help recharge and lift your spirits?
- Who leaves you feeling drained or worse after spending time with them?
- What are some fun or energizing activities you could introduce into your routine?
- What do you wish you had the time and energy to do for your students?
- How do you make time for self-care each day?

I hope the answers to these questions inspire you to find your own strategies for turning your days into good ones—even great ones.

Now, before I order a glass of red wine and a bowl of butternut squash soup, tell me more about your great day.

Part 2
The Little Details

Before We Begin ...

Before we dive in any further, let's clarify two important points. First, the only person you can truly change is yourself. This isn't new information, you know this, but do you live and behave like you know this? Second, we are surprisingly bad at knowing what makes us happy. I mean, flat out terrible.

If you're anything like me, accepting these truths can be difficult, and I say this reluctantly because I wish it weren't the case. I've often wanted to change others and believed that happiness was just around the corner if I looked hard enough. Unfortunately, it doesn't work that way. The sooner you embrace these truths, the better. Don't waste as much time as I did trying to change people or striving for things that I thought would make me happy.

Experience teaches you that in relationships, you can't change someone else. You can try, but it's often a fruitless endeavor. Instead, focus on changing yourself. Be the change you want to see in the world, in your school, and in your classroom. I promise, this approach is not only more effective but also far more rewarding.

As for happiness, let me illustrate what I mean. We often spend a lot of time chasing happiness, creating our own lists of what we think will bring us joy. But if we reflect on the past instead of looking ahead, we may realize we're often pursuing the wrong things. Think about the last time you felt truly happy—even if just for a moment. Was it something you meticulously planned? Did it come from crossing something off your "I wish I had this" list?

Was it tied to hitting a certain weight or looking your best? Was it during a grand adventure or while receiving an award? I would venture to guess it was none of those.

As I sit here writing, I'm reflecting on my own recent moments of happiness, and one stands out vividly: watching our dog, Kate, pouncing like Tigger from *Winnie the Pooh*.[1] She was intent on catching a lizard that had scurried across our path. Her tail wagged in excitement as her nose dug into the earth, and I couldn't help but laugh. I pulled Kate into a warm hug and smiled. In that instant, I felt a wave of genuine happiness wash over me. All was right with the world—and the lizards.

Now, just so you know, I have recently lost a little weight, bought a beautiful home, been on a trip, and received an honor at work, but my answer to the happiness question was a random moment on a routine walk with my dog, Kate.

So, what should we chase if not the usual milestones and achievements? We should chase presence—the ability to be fully in the moment, to notice the small, beautiful details of daily life that so often slip by unnoticed. We should pursue connection, with ourselves and with others, fostering genuine relationships built on trust and care. And most of all, we should chase meaning, seeking out the values, actions, and purposes that align with who we truly are. Happiness, after all, isn't a finish line to reach; it's a byproduct of living with intention, authenticity, and openness. As Mark Manson writes in *The Subtle Art of Not Giving a F****, the desire for more positive experiences is itself a negative experience.[2] Embracing your struggles, rather than resisting them, becomes the first step toward the happiness you seek.

Here is the big picture: Taking the time to prioritize yourself isn't just beneficial—it's essential. By investing in your well-being, you'll not only reduce burnout but also show up as a stronger, more present educator for your students. It's a win-win that starts with small, intentional choices. While spectacular trips overseas, a beautiful home, a polished outfit, or professional accolades are wonderful, true fulfillment often comes from the little moments of joy woven into your daily life. Let's explore those moments together and discover simple, meaningful ways to nurture happiness at work, at home, and every day. ***Let's travel this road together—from burnout to bliss—one small, meaningful step at a time.***

7 How Can Email Improve Community?

Since many of us begin our days by checking our email, it's a fitting place to begin our journey. Email is a vital part of our professional lives, influencing our productivity and relationships—both positively and negatively. So, how can email help us lessen our burnout? How can we harness this tool to improve our work experience?

Let's look at the first question. One way to lessen your burnout is to take steps in a positive direction. They don't have to be big steps—just big enough to feel some sense of accomplishment. As the ancient Chinese saying by Lao Tzu goes, "The journey of a thousand miles begins with one single step."[1]

Here are some practical tips to enhance your email communication and strengthen workplace relationships. While these suggestions won't solve every challenge, they can help foster a more positive and collaborative environment for you, your colleagues, and your students. You can start implementing these strategies tomorrow morning when you check your inbox!

Tip #1: Choose Face-to-Face Conversations When Possible

Whenever you can have a personal conversation instead of sending an email, opt for that. Nothing builds relationships and community quite like spending time together in person. Plus, direct interactions reduce the risk of misinterpretation and help convey your tone more clearly. This is especially effective if the subject of your conversation is sensitive in any way.

Another advantage of face-to-face conversations is that they encourage you to step away from your computer and your desk. You might even enjoy some fresh air or a pleasant little walk in the process!

Let me challenge you even more. Is there someone's email you need to reply to that you don't know very well? Why not start there? The research supports this idea. Two new studies found that connecting with someone in person is even nicer than we expect it to be.[2] And, these studies go along with other research, suggesting that we don't have a good sense of how pleasurable it is for others to connect with us.[3] See, we really don't know what makes us happy.

Tip #2: Every Email You Receive Is an Opportunity to Say Something Kind

If you can, add a positive comment to each email you send. Make sure it is appropriate and authentic, but view each email as a chance to compliment and support the teachers and students you are working with. Here is an example:

> *Dear Susie,*
>
> *Thank you for your email to reschedule your test. I am glad you are advocating so well for yourself and taking care of this in a timely manner. Your suggestion of taking the test during your study hall today is perfect. I will have the test there and ready for you.*
>
> *Thank you again for your dedication to this class. Your hard work is not going unnoticed.*
>
> *Have a great day,*
>
> *Mrs. McDowell*

Tip #3: Make It a Habit to Scroll Back Through Your Inbox

You will be grateful for the second look at your emails. It will surprise you how much you miss on the first pass. Make this a daily practice, whether it's before your day begins or just before you head home. Scroll back through all the emails from the day or the day before. While you might initially hesitate to add anything to your daily routine, the payoff will be worthwhile. Now, you can confidently say you're no longer anxious about missing important messages—the peace of mind you gain is truly worth the minor adjustment.

Tip #4: Never Hit REPLY ALL and Never Send Long Emails

Unless you are asked to do so by the author of the original email, never hit reply all. It just causes trouble. You can help people *unpopulate* their inboxes by resisting this urge. You also reduce the risk of embarrassing yourself.

Also, never send a long email. It will not be completely read by everyone. If you have a lot to say, try bullet points. Be as clear and concise as you can be. People will appreciate your respect for their time.

Tip #5: Inject Some Fun!

Start with the subject. Can you creatively say what you need to say and make someone smile at the same time? This is a good goal to work toward. Instead of Faculty Agenda, try *Unlocking the Secrets of the Faculty Fortress: Your Agenda Awaits!* If you have a passion for puns or love to quote movie one-liners, why not bring that into your emails? Instead of Weekly Dorm Duty Schedule, try *Dorm Duty: The Ultimate Game of Who Can Stay Awake!*

And, who knew the lost and found could be so entertaining? At school, misplaced water bottles, lone sneakers, and forgotten hoodies are a daily saga. Normally, a simple email would suffice to track them down—but one teacher decided to turn this everyday task into a comedic art form. Rather than sending dull reminders, he unleashed a series of witty, over-the-top emails claiming his "world-class detective skills" in tracking down rogue backpacks and runaway lunch boxes. His messages became so hilarious that faculty members started looking forward to them. "I love his emails," one teacher confessed. "They actually make my day!"

He didn't stop there. With his newfound reputation as the school's unofficial "lost and found" celebrity, he took his playful approach even further. During the holiday season, he launched a competition among the dorms to find the elusive *Elf on the Shelf*, adding an extra layer of fun and excitement to the usual holiday cheer. His emails became a delightful highlight of the school year, blending humor with a bit of holiday magic.

Another way to have fun is how you sign off your emails. Some people have deep philosophical quotes, and some people take a lighter route. Here is a fan-favorite for sign-offs: "Like a unicorn, I'm off to spread magic elsewhere." During COVID, this one brought a smile to everyone's face: "Hope you're staying positive and testing negative." I am sure you can come up with something that will make someone laugh! And, as a mathematics teacher, how can you not appreciate this quote? "A day without Math is like … Just kidding, I have no idea."

Tip#6: Use the *Delay-Send* Option on Your Email

Did you know you can set a delay before your emails are sent? Unlike the scheduled send option, which requires you to set it each time, this feature applies automatically every time you hit send. It gives your computer a brief pause—anywhere from a few seconds to a minute—allowing you to cancel the send if you notice a mistake or want to make changes. You can customize the delay to fit your needs.

This feature can save you. It feels like there's a helpful guardian in your computer, always looking out for you. It's nice knowing someone or something has your back. Give it a try—you might be pleasantly surprised by how much it helps!

Tip #7: Listen to Einstein

Albert Einstein once said, "It has become appallingly obvious that our technology has exceeded our humanity." Let this be a reminder to make it a personal goal for this never to be true for you. While technology is an essential part of our lives and offers countless advantages, it's crucial not to lose sight of the importance of personal connections. Strive to keep your humanity at the forefront, ensuring that technology enhances rather than replaces the bonds that truly matter.

Before we wrap up this chapter, I want to make sure you fully understand what the research is revealing about you. People genuinely enjoy your company more than either you or they might realize. So, stop sending so many emails and see if you can create some enjoyable in-person connections.

8 *Have You Ever Thought About What You Can Do Before the Learning Begins?*

Before you watch Dr. Kerry Howells's TED Talk, "How Thanking Awakens Our Thinking," you may never have considered the importance of preparing your students' mindset before teaching even begins.[1] Her talk will challenge you to reflect on the power of focusing on a central, guiding question in your teaching practice. Dr. Howells believes that every teacher should have a quintessential question to explore and enhance their teaching, and her own question is, "What does it mean to be truly awake?" It was by answering this question that she discovered the power of preparing students to learn.

Through her research, Dr. Howells highlights three key insights. First, she discovered that students want to be "awake" in their learning but often don't know how to achieve that state. Second, many teachers don't view it as their responsibility to "wake up" their students, nor do they feel equipped to do so. Finally, Dr. Howells notes that we have become complacent, settling for a low level of engagement and awareness in our students.

To combat this problem, Dr. Howells suggests we use the power of gratitude. Believe it or not, a grateful mindset helps us learn. In addition to that, according to the research done by Daniel Kahneman in his book *Thinking Fast and Slow*, being in a good mood increases cognitive skills.[2] So, what can we do with this wonderful information?

Before we dive in, let's take a moment to appreciate the significance of this research. It's truly enlightening. By fostering gratitude and a positive mood, we can boost our students' engagement and cognitive function. Not only will this create an environment for authentic learning to take place, but ideally, it will make the learning experience more enjoyable for both us and our students. If you're anything like me, this is the kind of insight that reignites our faith in the power of teaching and helps us stay motivated in our work.

So, how do we achieve this goal? The answer lies with you. It's about finding an authentic way to weave gratitude and positivity into your teaching routine. It could be something as simple as sharing a lighthearted joke, thanking your students for something they are doing well, starting the class with a brief mindfulness exercise, or telling a personal story. You'll need to discover what resonates most with you and your students.

For example, if you share a classroom with another teacher, a gratitude board may not work. But a thoughtfully chosen quote at the beginning of each lesson does. Pick quotes that are both uplifting and inspiring. Take a moment to plan this out *before* your lesson. The students enjoy reading the quotes, and the conversations they spark are often just as valuable as the content of the lesson itself. Some students even contribute their own favorite quotes, adding a personal touch to the environment.

You may find that there are times when you must rein in the "magic" and shift focus back to the task at hand—but even then, the positive energy lingers in the room, quietly influencing the atmosphere and interactions. The residual effects of that small act of gratitude carry far beyond the moment.

Even though this chapter's focus is on what we do before the learning begins, you need to go back and highlight Dr. Howells's idea of a quintessential question. This is too good of an idea to skip over. For Dr. Howells, it was the beginning of her research, and it got her to look at the fact that thanking and thinking come from the same word.[3] Her work has shown us that if "we thank before we think we learn better."[4]

So, what is your quintessential question? What question drives and defines your teaching practice? This is another big question. Maybe some other ones will help you come up with an answer. Here are some more questions to think about:

- What is most important to you in your classroom?
- What do you want your students to have and embrace while they are with you?

- What do you want your students to take away from your time together?
- What is most important about your content area, and what skills do your students need to truly immerse themselves and build a solid foundation?

Starting the learning process with reflection and gratitude can set a powerful tone for the day. Before diving into new material, take a moment to remind your students that their mindset plays a crucial role in how they learn. A growth-oriented, joyful attitude not only enhances understanding but also builds resilience and motivation. Let them know that by fostering thankfulness and joy, you're not just aiming to create a positive classroom atmosphere—you're intentionally helping them grow as learners and as individuals. The goal is not just to learn, but to learn joyfully and gratefully. This leads to better learning. How great is that!

9 How Can You Make Gratitude Your Superpower?

Believe it or not, teachers who regularly practice gratitude are less likely to experience burnout. They also report higher job satisfaction and feel less emotionally drained and exhausted.[1] These are some powerful findings! Which is why we added another chapter about gratitude.

It's important to note that gratitude is not something we're born with—it's a skill we need to cultivate and practice daily. But why should we put in the effort? Research shows that practicing gratitude enhances self-awareness, boosts self-management, and improves social awareness. It also strengthens our relationship skills and helps us make better, more responsible decisions. In addition, gratitude aids in stress management, regulates emotions, promotes overall health, nurtures relationships, and even energizes learning.[2]

Still Need More Reasons to Make Gratitude Part of Your Daily Routine?

Chevy Cheney and Pawan (Pav) Wander, middle school teachers from Toronto, Ontario, Canada, offer this insight: "We've come to understand that expressing gratitude with sincerity and intention—and equally, learning to receive it with genuine appreciation—is essential to effective teaching and to creating meaningful, lasting learning environments."[3]

So, What Is Gratitude?

There are many definitions of gratitude, but they all center around two key ideas: first, recognizing something worthy of thanks, and second, acknowledging the person or force behind the positive act. True gratitude goes beyond simply appreciating the good; it also involves recognizing the efforts of those—typically people—who played a role in bringing that good into your life.

According to Lainie Rowell, in her book *Evolving with Gratitude*, gratitude is on a spectrum from simple reciprocity to a grateful disposition.[4] As you develop a grateful disposition, you can keep yourself happier for longer.

> *Gratitude keeps us at a higher level of happiness for longer for two reasons: (1) when we are intentionally grateful for the good in our lives, we maintain joy rather than taking things for granted, and (2) practicing gratitude releases two happiness chemicals, serotonin and dopamine. These two feel-good chemical messengers are neurotransmitters that promote a happy mood and positive feelings.*[5]

Making gratitude part of your identity will increase your level of joy and increases your ability to learn. Imagine what it can do for your classroom. And, as Rowell says, "Showing gratitude and kindness are two of the best forms of self-care."[6]

Here are a few tips to help you establish a meaningful gratitude practice. First, start by recognizing and fully receiving acts of kindness. Stay open to the moments that invite you to feel grateful, whether big or small. Next, take action: there are countless ways to express gratitude, so find the ones that resonate most with you. If possible, bring gratitude into your classroom by modeling it and teaching it to your students. The positive impact it will have is well worth the effort and time.

Oprah is famous for suggesting that everyone keep a gratitude journal. Since this book isn't about you doing more, maybe that isn't the greatest suggestion, but thinking about what you are grateful for is still worth your time. When all your students walk in the door, think about what you are thankful for as you look over your class. You can even ask your students what they are grateful for. When you pack up and get ready to go home, think about what you are grateful for—even though you are probably exhausted and already thinking about dinner. Training yourself to take moments to reflect and show gratitude will help you cultivate a more grateful mindset.

It's important to remember that practicing gratitude doesn't mean you'll feel joyful all the time. That's not the goal, and it's not realistic. Don't use constant happiness as a yardstick for how grateful you are. Instead, commit to giving gratitude a try for a week and see if it brings value and joy to your life.

Finally, a key thought to keep in mind as you embrace gratitude in both your personal and professional life: understand that the opposite of gratitude is entitlement. As educators, we often encounter signs of entitlement in students, and we make efforts to address them. By consistently practicing and modeling gratitude, we offer a powerful antidote to entitlement—creating a win-win situation for both us and our students.

10 How Do You Always Assume Good Intent?

Many schools invite their seniors to deliver speeches in the spring of their final year. These speeches are often seen as a heartfelt gift to the community they are about to leave behind. While not every senior partakes in this tradition, those who do offer us something truly special. It's always inspiring to hear words of wisdom, especially from students you've had the privilege to teach. These speeches provide a glimpse into what students value and hold dear.

Ginger was no exception. Her senior speech in Chapel was unforgettable, and the central message she shared was one that resonated deeply: *always assume good intent with everyone you interact with.*[1] She learned this lesson from her dad, and it became one of her guiding principles. It was simple, yet powerful advice—one that clearly brought her joy. It was no surprise, given that Ginger was one of the warmest, funniest, and kindest people on campus, radiating both humor and goodwill. Could it really be that the key to a happy life was so straightforward?

When we assume good intent, we treat people the way we want to be treated. We limit our judgment and allow them space to be who they truly are. Assuming good intent isn't easy, and it is not a skill you perfect. It also may get you burned, but it is still worth the effort. It seems like you are doing it for them, but really it is for you. When you assume good intent and look for the good in others, you will naturally become happier. You will soften, and life will become more enjoyable. Try it. See what happens. Ginger knows what she is talking about.

How do you assume good intent? It starts by forgiving others before they make mistakes. It's about defending someone before they even realize they need defending. It's standing by their side before they feel the weight of being alone. When someone raises their voice, instead of reacting with anger, recognize that they might be facing challenges and struggling. Respond with empathy and kindness. When someone speaks behind your back, choose to forgive them—they're likely going through something difficult.

It's not always easy, is it? But it truly can be. As humans, we're wired to assume the worst. But when we do that, it harms us and our relationships. It clouds the way we view the world and others. We need to shift this mindset because it's not just about being kind—it's about protecting our peace and nurturing deeper connections. It will take time and practice, but what you are aiming for is a moment to stop and not react with emotion. You are aiming to give yourself an opportunity to assume good intent. This is a wonderful way to build a community you want to work in and be a part of.

Assuming good intent when working with colleagues who challenge you can be difficult, but it's an important skill to develop. Remember, this practice benefits you just as much—if not more—than it benefits them. When tensions arise, try to shift your perspective. If there's a teacher you don't always see eye-to-eye with, start there. Consider their experiences, motivations, and the possibility that their intentions are rooted in what they believe is best.

Likewise, if you find yourself at odds with an administrator who has a different vision, challenge yourself to assume they are acting in good faith. Their perspective, while different from yours, may come from a broader view of the school's needs or long-term goals.

This shift in mindset doesn't mean you have to agree with them or ignore valid frustrations, but it allows for more productive conversations, stronger professional relationships, and a more positive work environment. It's not always easy, but it's worth the effort.

Let's take this one step further—into the classroom. As educators, we must always assume good intent with our students. It's essential to create a supportive learning environment. Embracing a growth mindset means believing in each student's potential and assuming good intent, no matter the circumstance. These aren't just ideals; they are non-negotiable parts of being a teacher. When we fail to do so, we risk doing more harm than good. It's crucial that we approach every student with understanding, trust, and a belief in their ability to grow. That is another way of saying *assume good intent.*

This means we must ensure our expectations are clear, communicate effectively with each student, and demonstrate that we genuinely care. This demeanor allows us to walk alongside our students through their challenges—offering guidance, support, and encouragement—we help them navigate difficulties with the confidence that growth and success await on the other side. When students know they are not alone, they are more likely to persevere, take academic risks, and develop the resilience needed to overcome obstacles. We assume good intent to help them grow.

11 How Do You Reclaim Joy?

Considering the two key insights we started with—that we can only change ourselves and that we often struggle to identify what truly brings us happiness—how can we effectively combat burnout? One powerful solution lies in reclaiming joy. Rather than waiting for joy to find us, we must actively seek it out and make it a daily practice. As theologian Henri Nouwen wisely said, "Joy does not simply happen to us. We have to choose joy and keep choosing it every day."[1] But what does that look like in practice?

Before we can reclaim joy, we must first recognize what is stealing joy from us. What leaves you feeling drained, frustrated, or disheartened? Identifying these culprits is the first step in taking back control. Is it constant disappointment? An overwhelming workload? A negative self-image? Unhealthy comparisons? While it may be unrealistic to eliminate every source of stress, increasing awareness of these triggers allows us to shift our perspective and take action where possible.

Once you know what is weighing you down, experiment with small, manageable changes that can help you reclaim joy. If a messy house adds to your stress, commit to a five-minute reset at the end of each day to create a sense of order. If the noise level in your classroom is overwhelming, introduce calming music or structured quiet moments to create a more peaceful environment. If negative self-image dims your confidence, stand in front of a mirror and find three things you appreciate about your appearance. The goal isn't perfection—it's learning to redirect your focus toward the positive. Joy isn't about grand, sweeping life changes. It's about small, intentional choices that build upon one another, creating a ripple effect of positivity. Even the act of trying can shift your mindset and energy. And, with practice, choosing joy becomes more natural.

Another powerful tool for reclaiming joy, as we have already said, is gratitude. Understand, the more we train ourselves to look for things to appreciate, the more we will begin to see them. Even in the most chaotic seasons of life, there is always something to be grateful for—it just takes intentionality to recognize it with consistency. Gratitude has a way of grounding us, pulling us out of stress and exhaustion, and shifting our focus toward what is good, toward joy.

Reclaiming joy is more than just a luxury—it's a necessity, especially in a profession as emotionally demanding as teaching. Beyond improving your emotional well-being, joy has a profound impact on the brain. When you experience joy, your mind is flooded with positive chemicals like dopamine and serotonin, which help counteract stress responses, boost resilience, and foster a sense of balance and renewal. Think about this: looking for and seeing the joy in your life can benefit you as much as a physical workout. The health benefits are more than you can imagine.

For educators, joy isn't just about fleeting moments of happiness; it's deeply tied to purpose and meaning. It's found in the quiet triumphs—the moment a struggling student finally grasps a difficult concept, the spark of curiosity in a child's eyes, or the heartfelt "thank you" from a student who sees their own potential because of you. These moments, though small, build up over time, strengthening your motivation and reinforcing why you chose this path in the first place. These moments build up your resilience and take away your burnout.

However, joy doesn't just happen; it requires intentionality. Burnout creeps in when exhaustion and frustration overshadow the moments that once inspired you. To reclaim joy, you must make a conscious effort to notice, savor, and celebrate these moments. Whether it's through gratitude, reflection, or simply allowing yourself to pause and appreciate the impact you're making, prioritizing joy can transform the way you experience your work. And if you can experience your work in a more positive way, then you are on your way to becoming a happier teacher and a better version of yourself.

Reclaiming joy isn't about ignoring the challenges—it's about finding light within them. It's about recognizing that joy is not just a feeling but a source of strength, renewal, and motivation to keep going, even on the hardest days. And that is worth every bit of effort, especially if burnout is taking its toll on your soul.

12 Did You Ever Think That Doing Less Would Be Better for Your Students?

The idea that simplicity can be more powerful than excess appears frequently in Shakespeare's writing. How can we apply that wisdom to the classroom? (Did you catch that? A math teacher referencing Shakespeare.)

Indulge me for a moment. Think back to a lesson that didn't go as well as you'd hoped. What did you do afterward? Chances are, you reflected, identified areas for improvement, and put in significant effort to ensure the next lesson would go better. You probably also took it personally—viewed it as a failure and vowed to do better. But did you ever consider the role your students might have played in this? Perhaps the lesson didn't go as planned, not because of something you did, but because of something your students did—or didn't do.

I'm not suggesting we assign blame, but as teachers, we often have a tendency to shoulder the responsibility ourselves. We rewrite lesson plans, rethink our delivery, and search for ways to make the material more engaging. But let's explore another possibility: maybe it wasn't all on you. Maybe the students had a role in their own learning experience.

Sometimes, when we take on more than our fair share in the classroom, we unintentionally hinder our students' growth. In our effort to make learning easier for them, we can end up doing the heavy lifting ourselves. But true teaching isn't about making things effortless for students—it's about guiding them toward independence, accountability, and resilience.

So, how do we achieve this? One of the most effective approaches is to shift responsibility back where it belongs. If you notice a lack of student engagement, don't just work harder—bring it to their attention. If students aren't taking advantage of extra help, discuss this with them. Learning is a two-way street. Simply making things easier for them might bring temporary relief, but it does not equip them with the skills they need to improve. Our role is to support, challenge, and guide—not to carry them through every struggle.

Another area where we need to embrace "less" is in the expectations we place on ourselves. We don't need to be the first to arrive and the last to leave. Who decided that schedule was the key to teaching success? A tired teacher, that's who. We need balance—because if we want to bring our best selves into the classroom, we must take care of ourselves first.

And here's another radical idea: If you're sick, stay home. Don't try to be a hero. Practically speaking, you could be contagious. Professionally speaking, you need rest. Teaching while exhausted or unwell doesn't serve you or your students. Yes, you may fall behind for a day. But when you return recharged, you'll be in a much better place to handle whatever comes next. And, you have modeled self-care for your students and your colleagues.

At its core, this is about a shift in perspective. To be the best teacher you can be, you must prioritize yourself. Take good care—because a well-cared-for teacher is a more effective, inspired, and present teacher. This is the missing piece for so many of us. We are so focused on the needs of others that we forget about our own—let alone our own desires. We think that just because we can do something, we should. Sometimes we need to let go and have others do the work. This could be students, and this could be colleagues. A student can explain a concept to the class or answer another student's question. A colleague can cover a class for you while you take the time to regain your health. In these moments, let go and let others help. It is hard and it takes practice, but it is essential to your well-balanced life.

One of the clearest symptoms of burnout is feeling like we have nothing left to give. But here's the truth: we can't give endlessly if we're not replenishing ourselves. Doing less isn't about neglecting your work—it's about working smarter, letting students take ownership of their learning, and allowing yourself the space to breathe. When we do this, we don't just help ourselves—we help our students, too.

Less can be more. And in teaching, that might just be the lesson we all need the most.

13 Why Is Accountability Important to Community?

Accountability provides numerous benefits for schools. It drives overall improvement, fosters a community of trust, and plays a more significant role in decision making than many realize. Additionally, accountability promotes motivation, personal responsibility, and progress toward success. It also helps prevent the abuse of power and ensures equality. Despite its many advantages, not all schools prioritize or practice professional accountability, leading to severe consequences, such as teacher burnout. Being aware of this can help you understand your frustrations and disenchantment with your school and with teaching. Remember, we are not trying to change our schools, we just want to help ourselves.

If your school doesn't value accountability, your job will be more difficult than it should be. How can you tell if this is the case? Start by examining the workload—Is it distributed fairly? When school events take place, does everyone contribute? If someone neglects their responsibilities, can you trust that the issue will be addressed promptly and effectively? If you answered no to any of these questions, your school may need to reevaluate how it holds it teachers accountable but that isn't what we are going to focus on. Instead of focusing on what others should do, let's focus on what you can control—your own accountability.

The solution is simple: do the work—all of it. Attend meetings when required. Show up for crosswalk duty on time. If you're responsible for the faculty room coffee, make sure there's good coffee. Holding yourself accountable not only ensures you meet expectations, but it also gives you the satisfaction of doing the right thing—without the guilt of cutting corners. More importantly, it sets the right example for students. Show up—that's half the battle.

Another thing a lack of accountability does is stifle innovation because good ideas won't gain traction when there's no confidence that the work will be carried through. This creates a stagnant school environment, where progress is slow, and frustration grows. Ultimately, accountability starts at the top. If leadership fails to uphold its faculty and staff accountable, the school's success is compromised, and your job becomes even more challenging and let's face it, less fun. Innovation is an important ingredient for learning. Without it, a love of learning and growing cannot thrive.

Consider this: We work hard to hold our students accountable for their actions and learning because we know it's essential for their growth. We encourage them to take ownership of their work, meet deadlines, and learn from their mistakes. But shouldn't we hold ourselves to the same standard?

Accountability isn't just something we teach—it's something we must embody. When we avoid responsibilities or push commitments aside, the work doesn't disappear. It lingers, piling up until it becomes overwhelming. Procrastination creates more stress in the long run, drains our energy, and fosters negativity. Worse yet, it sets an unspoken example for our students, subtly reinforcing the idea that cutting corners is acceptable.

The best way to show up for your students, your colleagues, and most importantly, yourself is simple: do the work and do it well. That doesn't mean perfection—it means consistency, effort, and integrity. When you hold yourself accountable, you build trust, credibility, and a deep sense of professional pride. You create a classroom culture where responsibility isn't just expected of students—it's modeled by their teacher.

So, set the bar high—not just for them, but for yourself. Take pride in your work, follow through on commitments, and face challenges head-on. Accountability isn't a burden; it's a foundation for success. When we hold ourselves to a high standard, we don't just become better educators—we become the kind of role models our students truly need.

Believe it or not, embracing this mindset will help you enjoy your job more. When you hold yourself accountable, take pride in your work, and commit to continuous growth, teaching becomes more than just a job—it becomes a fulfilling vocation. You'll feel a deeper sense of purpose, knowing that your efforts are making a real impact, and you are doing all you can to do what is best for your students.

If you're struggling to hold yourself accountable in certain areas of your job, don't be afraid to lean on a trusted colleague for support. Accountability isn't just about personal discipline—it's also about creating a culture of mutual encouragement and growth. Likewise, if you notice a colleague facing challenges, you can offer the same support in return.

Sometimes, accountability is as simple as having someone check in on your progress or help you push through procrastination. Other times, it requires deeper conversations—exploring what's holding you back, identifying obstacles, and finding solutions together. Seeking help isn't a sign of weakness; it's a powerful way to improve both individually and collectively.

By holding each other accountable, you not only strengthen your own commitment but also contribute to a positive, growth-oriented community. Teaching is demanding work, but when we lift each other up, we make it a little easier—and a lot more fulfilling.

14 How Can You Celebrate More in Your Classroom?

There is an elementary school teacher in Vermont who hand-knits mittens for her students when they master their multiplication tables through the twelves. Can you picture it? A playground full of children playing in the snow, their hands wrapped in colorfully vibrant, one-of-a-kind mittens, each stitch a testament to their hard work. A teacher at a boarding school in Massachusetts hosts an annual tea party for the girls in her dorm, complete with elegant hats, fancy tea sets, and tasty biscuits. For one afternoon, they laugh, sip tea, and experience a moment of simple, royal joy.

What Unique Way Can You Celebrate Your Students?

Sometimes, the most meaningful celebrations are deeply personal—not just to the teacher, but to the student. A teacher in Florida, determined to support a student who frequently missed school due to medical treatments, found an unexpected way to lift his spirits. Knowing he loved sports, she created a Super Bowl Square Pool just for the class. Everyone put their name in five of the squares. There was no betting—only sweet treats awarded at the end of each quarter, which, in true classroom camaraderie, were shared by all the day the student returned.

Celebrations don't need to be extravagant to be effective. In fact, the simplest ones often leave the biggest impact. A high school science teacher in New York rewards his students after their grueling Advanced Placement exam by making homemade fudge—a sweet ending to months of hard work. A kindergarten teacher in Minnesota transforms her classroom into a smoothie bar, using the opportunity to teach her students about different fruits and vegetables while blending up a delicious, hands-on lesson. A middle school teacher in Virginia marks the 100th day of school with a special reflection exercise. Students celebrate their progress, set goals for the rest of the school year, and invite parents to see their accomplishments displayed throughout the classroom. They also have fun with the number 100 by writing it in different languages and representing the number in different ways.

You don't have to look far to find creative, heartfelt ways to celebrate your students. These moments aren't just fun; they build community, inspire motivation, and create lasting memories. Often, the anticipation of a celebration is just as powerful as the event itself. For some students, a seemingly small recognition can be life-changing.

One student, after winning a high school poetry contest, credited that experience as the moment she saw herself as a writer. Years later, she became a published poet, frequently reflecting on how that classroom competition helped shape her identity and future. Her prize, a framed photo of the class, is one of her most valued possessions.

Of course, there are always reasons not to celebrate. Maybe things aren't perfect. Maybe there's still room for improvement. But that's exactly the point—celebrations don't have to mark the final destination. They can acknowledge progress, perseverance, and the determination to keep going. Some might say life is too hard for celebrations, that they seem frivolous when times are tough. But joy isn't frivolous—it's essential. Even in the hardest moments, there is always the possibility for joy. So, find it and celebrate it.

A teacher in New Hampshire makes his famous mint brownies for his AP English class once everyone brings in a college rejection letter. In Connecticut, there is a teacher who teaches his students to play backgammon. Once everyone can play, he challenges his students to play against him. If anyone can beat him, he will take the entire class to lunch. They put aside class time on Friday afternoons to play.

And if cost is a concern? Ask for help. Scale it down. The size of the celebration isn't what matters—it's the meaning behind it.

In the end, what students will remember most is not the test scores, the homework, or the long lectures. They will remember how they felt. They will remember the teacher who saw them, believed in them, and took the time to celebrate their journey.

Still need more reasons to celebrate? Consider this: Recognizing achievements—both big and small—can be a powerful antidote to burnout. Celebrations boost morale, reduce stress, and create a sense of accomplishment that fuels motivation. When students and teachers alike feel valued and recognized, it cultivates a more positive and energized classroom environment. Not only does this reinforce hard work and perseverance, but it also fosters a culture of encouragement and resilience. Small moments of celebration can spark joy, strengthen relationships, and inspire an optimistic outlook for the future—making the learning journey more fulfilling for everyone. So, how will you celebrate your students and yourself?

15 How Can Storytelling Enrich Your Classroom?

Why not reward your students with a story? Stories have the power to engage, inspire, and connect. They can bring a lesson to life, provide a fresh perspective, or reveal a part of yourself that helps students see you as more than just their teacher. A well-told story can be humorous, motivational, or even thought-provoking—drawing students in and making the learning experience more memorable.

The power of storytelling is an untapped resource in many classrooms, yet it has the ability to break down barriers, spark curiosity, and create an emotional connection to the material. A story can make abstract concepts tangible, help students relate to challenges and triumphs, and reinforce key lessons in ways traditional instruction cannot or falls short.

So, how can you harness this power? When used effectively, storytelling doesn't just entertain—it educates, resonates, and inspires. In Rob Biesenbach's book, *Unleash the Power of Storytelling: Win Hears, Change Minds, Get Results*, he says, "In an age of information overload, stories rise above the noise and intensify the impact of your ideas."[1] And, storytelling isn't as hard as you think. Here are more of Biesenbach's quotes to persuade you to become a storyteller:

> "If you want to break down walls with people, truly connect with them, and make an impact, few things beat a well-crafted, well-told story."[2]

"Multiple studies show that stories have a unique effect on our brains." As far as the brain is concerned, there is little difference between a story and an event.[3]

A good story possesses several key qualities that make it compelling and impactful. First, stories tap into emotion, allowing audiences to feel deeply connected to the narrative. They also put a face on an issue, making abstract or complex topics more relatable and understandable. Additionally, stories have the power to connect us, fostering a sense of shared experience and unity. They humanize us, revealing the depth of our experiences and emotions in ways that facts alone cannot. Furthermore, great stories raise the stakes, creating tension and investment in the outcome. Finally, storytelling is about showing rather than telling, using vivid details, actions, and experiences to bring the narrative to life rather than simply stating facts. In its simplest form, a story is a character in pursuit of a goal and faces some challenges or obstacles. How the character tries to resolve the issue drives the narrative.

To make a story truly work, several key issues must be addressed. First, the character should feel real and relatable, allowing the audience to connect with them on a personal level. Additionally, there must be sufficient conflict to drive the narrative forward and keep readers engaged. The stakes should also be high enough to create tension and make the outcome feel meaningful. A strong story requires clear cause and effect, ensuring that each event logically follows from the previous one. Finally, at the heart of every compelling story is an emotional core, providing depth and resonance that leave a lasting impact on the audience.

As for the structure of a story, most stories have a beginning, middle, and end. Simply put, the beginning sets a scene and introduces the characters. Once that is done, an enticing incident sets the story in motion. The middle is where the characters work to overcome the challenge, and the end is where things come to a resolution—not always a happy ending, but maybe a lesson learned.

Creating a pedagogically effective story requires following a few basic steps. First, it is essential to know your audience (students) and understand who they are. Next, determine the goal—what you want the audience to do or take away from the story. Consider the challenges that need to be addressed, as these will shape the narrative's conflict and stakes. Then, find a character who has faced and overcome that challenge, making the story relatable and engaging. If it can be you, that is even better. Finally, ensure there is a clear resolution, providing closure and reinforcing the message or lesson of the story.

Facts don't fuel action the way a story—an emotional appeal does. Emotion unlocks action. Your job as a storyteller is to provoke an emotional reaction. To do that, exhibit emotion yourself. Tell your story well and build up the drama if you can.

When you are formulating your stories, make sure there's an emotional component that will help you break down walls and create common ground with your students. Have a good reason for telling your story in the first place.

Tap into loyalty, appeal to pride, and celebrate your heroes—because students crave a personal connection with their teachers. Opening up and revealing your humanity isn't just encouraged; it's part of your job. When you share stories that grab your students' hearts, you build that connection and deepen their engagement. Stories not only inspire, they also explain the "why" behind the "what," providing the rationale for policies and practices. They move students beyond mere compliance and toward genuine buy-in.

When crafting a story, it is just as important to consider what to leave out as it is to decide what to include. Start with a clear goal to keep the narrative focused and eliminate unnecessary characters who don't serve the story's purpose. Avoid tangents—storytelling should flow like a tree growing from the trunk to the top, rather than branching off in too many directions. Steer clear of unnecessary turning points that distract from the main message. Be selective with details, using all five senses when possible but simplifying dates, making numbers more meaningful, and omitting proper nouns when they don't add value. Cut excessive exposition to maintain engagement. And remember, it's okay to tweak minor details as long as the essence of the story remains true—a good rule of thumb is to ask, would someone who was there still recognize your story?

The worst time to look for a story is when you need one, so it's important to have a system for finding and storing them. Use your goals and priorities as a filter to identify compelling narratives. Keep your antenna up, always staying alert for interesting stories in everyday life. Read and explore to discover new perspectives. Interview others to uncover personal insights and experiences. Draw from your own life to make stories authentic and relatable. Finally, find a way to store and organize your stories so they're ready when you need them.

Oh, and one last thing. Practice your stories. You can do this in front of a mirror, with a colleague, or a family member. Be sure that you know what you want to say and say it intentionally. Going off on tangents isn't what is best for a classroom setting. You can be casual and relaxed, but your message and your story are well rehearsed.

Are you convinced yet? Why not try telling a story tomorrow or tell your students you will reward them with a story soon?

16 Do You Do Research for Student Comments?

When writing student comments, your primary goal is to ensure that families feel their child is truly known—not just as a set of grades, but as an individual. Of course, academic progress is important, but parents and guardians also want reassurance that their child is seen, valued, and understood. A meaningful comment goes beyond test scores and assignments; it reflects the student's personality, work habits, and growth throughout the year.

So, how do you make sure your comments reflect this level of understanding?

Research

Take the time throughout the semester to observe and gather insights about each student. This doesn't need to be a daunting task, but a little intentional effort goes a long way. Keep a notebook or a digital file where you jot down small but significant details—how a student approaches challenges, the way they contribute to discussions, or moments when they show resilience or creativity. If a student has a unique way of solving problems, a habit of helping peers, or a newfound confidence in a subject, make a note of it. These details will enrich your comments and make them more personal and meaningful.

Another valuable strategy is to involve students in the process. Encourage them to reflect on their own learning by sharing their challenges, successes, and goals throughout the year. This can be done through self-assessments, classroom discussions, or even quick check-ins. When students articulate their own growth, it not only deepens their learning but also gives you richer material to include in your comments.

By being proactive and gathering insights consistently, you ensure that when it's time to write your student comments, the words will flow naturally.

Instead of struggling to recall details, you'll have a wealth of information that makes each comment feel authentic and personal—because it is.

One way to assess whether you have enough meaningful insight to write strong student comments is to do a quick mental check: Can you think of at least one or two things about each student that go beyond their grades? If you can describe their work habits, positive traits, interaction skills, or even how they perceive themselves as learners, then you are in great shape. However, if you find yourself struggling to recall anything beyond test scores and assignments, that's a sign you need to gather more information.

The ability to include specific anecdotes or concrete examples makes student comments far more impactful. Parents and guardians can quickly tell the difference between a thoughtfully written comment and a generic statement. Broad, vague remarks without supporting details may leave families feeling that their child is just another name on a roster rather than a unique individual in your classroom. Instead, referencing specific moments—like when a student demonstrated perseverance on a challenging project, showed kindness to a peer, or gained confidence in speaking up—adds authenticity and depth to your feedback.

Aside from doing research, another valuable strategy is to write your comments alongside a colleague. This collaborative approach offers multiple benefits, making the process smoother, more effective, and even enjoyable.

First, working with another teacher fosters a sense of camaraderie and support. Teaching is demanding, and comment-writing often comes at the busiest times of the year. Sitting down with a colleague can make the task feel less isolating and more manageable. When you have someone to share the workload with, the process becomes more engaging, helping both of you stay motivated and on track.

Second, collaboration provides a valuable sounding board for refining your comments. Sometimes, you may struggle with tone—wondering if a statement sounds too harsh or if your feedback could be framed in a more constructive way. A colleague can offer fresh perspectives, helping you ensure your message is both clear and supportive. They may also be familiar with some of your students and can contribute additional insights that strengthen your comments.

When it's your turn to help your colleague with their student comments, you gain a fresh perspective on the comment-writing process—one that can be both insightful and eye-opening. Stepping into the role of a listener and note-taker allows you to observe how another teacher thinks about their students, structures their feedback, and highlights student strengths and areas for growth. This outside perspective can help you refine your own approach, giving you new ideas for how to frame comments, balance honesty with encouragement, and make your feedback more personal and meaningful.

Additionally, hearing how a colleague describes their students may spark inspiration for your own writing. You might notice effective ways they phrase things, strategies they use to convey both praise and constructive feedback, or even small details they include to make comments feel more personal. This process not only strengthens your comment-writing skills but also reinforces the collaborative nature of teaching—reminding you that you don't have to do everything alone.

By engaging in this back-and-forth support system, you create a partnership that benefits both of you. You gain confidence in your own ability to craft meaningful feedback, while also helping your colleague do the same. In the end, this mutual exchange leads to stronger, more thoughtful comments that truly reflect each student's individuality and progress.

Finally, working together allows you to dictate comments while your colleague writes them down for you. This technique, if you haven't tried it, can be surprisingly effective. Speaking your thoughts aloud often helps you articulate ideas more naturally, and having someone transcribe them allows you to focus on clarity and detail without getting bogged down in typing or structure. This method can be especially useful when you're feeling stuck or unsure how to phrase something, or when you are short on time.

Thoughtful, well-crafted comments also serve as valuable PR within your school community. While you may not write them expecting a response, parents and guardians often appreciate insightful, personalized feedback. When they express their gratitude, those words of appreciation can be a meaningful reminder of the impact you have, helping you to see that you too are valued and needed.

Writing student comments doesn't have to be a tedious, solitary task—in fact, it can be a powerful tool in combating burnout and building colleagueship. By taking a proactive approach, you'll find that the effort you put in is well worth it, and you can turn a dreaded task into one that you enjoy.

17 Do You Remember Your Hobbies?

One of the great perks of being a teacher is the ability to bring your hobbies into the classroom. Whether you love animals, baking sourdough bread, or solving puzzles, you can find creative ways to incorporate your passions into your teaching.

Teachers who incorporate their passions into their lessons create engaging and memorable learning experiences for their students. For example, Mrs. Henry, a fourth-grade public school teacher in Virginia, with a deep love of history, brings the past to life in her classroom. She captivates her students with vivid stories about King Henry VIII—cleverly connecting to her own last name—and uses interactive discussions, role-playing activities, and creative projects to make history feel tangible and exciting.

Meanwhile, across the country in California, a high school math teacher with a love for crossword puzzles has found a clever way to blend logic, language, and problem-solving into the classroom. Each Thursday, students complete extra assignments as a challenge, earning the chance to collaboratively solve the previous Sunday's crossword puzzle as a class on Friday. This tradition not only strengthens critical thinking skills but also fosters teamwork and a love for learning in a fun and unconventional way. At first, it looks like a crossword puzzle has no business in a Precalculus class, but the collaboration, problem solving, and tenacity are needed and worthwhile skills.

By integrating their personal interests into their teaching, educators like Mrs. Henry and the math teacher in California create dynamic environments that inspire curiosity and engagement. Whether through history, puzzles, music, art, or any other passion, these personalized approaches help students connect with subjects in ways that feel meaningful and enjoyable.

By integrating their personal interests into lessons, teachers can make learning more engaging and meaningful for students. They can also use their hobbies to add an element of fun and provide a refreshing break from the daily routine. The beauty of this is that you can bring in what you love and enjoy your day even more.

If you're concerned about finding extra time in your schedule, consider starting an astronomy club or a lunchtime knitting group. If you're an athlete, explore opportunities to coach. There are countless ways to make your job more fulfilling while sharing your passions with students.

For example, a teacher in Massachusetts brought her love of yoga into the classroom, helping students manage anxiety—whether general stress or test-related nerves. By incorporating breathing exercises, stretching, and simple poses, she provided her students with valuable tools to stay focused and calm. She would often stop class, have everyone stand up, and go through a yoga flow of Mountain Pose, Forward Fold, Standing Backend, and then end in Warrior II.

What are your hobbies? How can you incorporate them into your classroom to create a more engaging learning environment? Your personal interests can be powerful tools for fostering creativity and enhancing student understanding.

If you enjoy drawing, consider integrating illustrations into your daily or weekly lessons. Visual elements can serve as study aids, spark curiosity, and help students retain information more effectively. For example, an AP Biology teacher encouraged her students to create and color detailed artwork on 11" × 17" paper, each piece representing a different human body system. This hands-on approach reinforced key concepts through visual learning, making complex topics more accessible.

To ensure that every student could participate, she provided templates for those who were less confident in their artistic skills. At the end of each chapter, the class would vote on their favorite illustration, and the winning piece would be framed and displayed on the classroom wall until the next chapter. This not only motivated students to engage deeply with the material but also fostered a sense of pride and accomplishment in their work.

By incorporating your passions into your teaching methods—whether through art, music, storytelling, or interactive projects—you can create a dynamic and personalized learning experience that resonates with your students.

In a creative effort to engage her students, an English teacher in New Hampshire developed a unique way to introduce each novel to her class. Before revealing the title of the next book they would read, she would draw a series of intriguing images on the board—symbols, characters, or key scenes—designed to hint at the story ahead. She then challenged her students to interpret the drawing and predict the book's themes, setting, or plot based on the visual clues.

As the class progressed through the novel, she would gradually add new details to the illustration, reflecting the unfolding narrative, pivotal moments, and character developments. By the time they reached the final chapter, the board displayed a rich and dynamic visual summary of the entire story—an artistic timeline that captured the essence of the book.

This interactive approach not only sparked curiosity and discussion but also helped students visualize literary elements, deepening their comprehension and engagement with the text. Her method turned reading into a collaborative and immersive experience, proving that sometimes, you really can judge a book by its cover—or, at least, by the evolving illustration on the classroom board.

Take a moment to look around your school and observe how teachers bring pieces of themselves into their classrooms and teaching styles. These personal touches—big or small—can make a powerful impact. You might already be doing this without even realizing it, or maybe you just need a little encouragement to lean in further.

It could be as simple as a passion for a sports team. Maybe you're a die-hard fan of your school's football or baseball team—bring that energy into your classroom! Decorate your space, talk up the games, and get your students hyped about school spirit. Or perhaps you're loyal to a professional team—let that fandom show. Hang up a poster, wear the jersey, and use game stats in your lessons. When students see what excites you, it gives them permission to be passionate, too.

More importantly, pay attention to what excites *them*. You might notice a group of students who are obsessed with skateboarding. That's not just a hobby—it's a cultural language. How can you tap into that? Can a lesson on physics explore momentum through tricks and flips? Can writing assignments dive into skate culture, or persuasive essays argue for a new skatepark?

The key is to meet students where they are—whether it's sports, music, gaming, anime, or something else entirely—and use those interests as bridges to deeper engagement and learning. When you open that door, what you gain in student connection, motivation, and creativity might just exceed your expectations.

Let your classroom reflect who you are. Encourage your students to do the same—and watch the magic that follows.

18 What Do Standardized Test Scores Really Tell Us?

You might recognize the value in standardized test scores. After all, there's an undeniable need for a way to compare student performance on a large scale. Teachers need accountability, and tests can provide a measure for that. However, you might also believe that we can do both accountability and student assessment better.

There are several aspects you may find problematic. For one, you might be deeply troubled by the multi-million-dollar industry that has grown around helping high school students improve their test scores. This industry only deepens the socioeconomic divide, offering an unfair advantage to those who can afford expensive test prep services. From an educational perspective, it does little to foster real learning or growth—not to mention a love of learning.

You may also strongly disagree with the practice of linking teacher pay to student performance on standardized tests. Consider this example: One year, I taught an AP Calculus AB class, with over forty students, and nearly every single one earned a five—an excellent result. But, a few years later, I taught another AP Calculus AB class of about forty students, and almost all of them scored a one. Same teacher, drastically different results. If my compensation had been tied to test outcomes, I would have been celebrated one year and condemned the next. This disparity underscores a fundamental flaw in using standardized test scores to determine a teacher's effectiveness or reward.

While these examples might seem extreme, they underscore a crucial point: standardized tests often overlook the complexities of teaching and learning. Never forget this fact—it can save you a great deal of frustration when reflecting on your own teaching journey. Yes, it's important to consider your students' scores, but always keep things in perspective. Don't let administrators or the local press misinterpret your students' results.

That said, this doesn't offer you a free pass. Instead, it serves as a reminder that there's always more to the story. Let me share a bit more about my experience. The year my students earned all fives, I was celebrated and praised for my work. However, I knew that the success was less about me and more about the incredible effort my hard-working students put in. I played a role, no doubt, but they carried the weight. This awareness helped me stay grounded, and it helped me celebrate my students.

After COVID when learning loss was a significant factor, it was no surprise that my students weren't prepared for the AP exam. Unfortunately, my school wasn't flexible in allowing them to opt out of the test. This was frustrating, but it ultimately helped me refocus on what mattered most. I knew my students wouldn't perform well on the test, and I was teaching a lot of Precalculus with and before the Calculus. I chose to meet them at their current level, prioritizing their growth over test scores. These students needed to learn the math they were ready for, to build a strong foundation that would prepare them for college and beyond, rather than rushing them through material that wasn't suited to their needs. I took a lot of flak for that year, but it was also one of the best teaching years of my career. The students in my class earned ones on the AP exam, but they also built a foundation that has served them well in their college Calculus courses.

One important aspect often overlooked in discussions about standardized tests is the emphasis on student improvement. For example, a student who moves from the 95th to the 98th percentile has made significant progress. However, many people might argue that a student who increases their score from the 50th to the 80th percentile has achieved even greater growth. This focus on improvement—rather than just the final score—is often missed by critics of teachers, who may fail to recognize the value of such progress.

So, what's the real takeaway here? Tune out the noise surrounding standardized testing and keep your focus where it truly matters—on your students and their growth. When conversations start revolving around test scores, remind yourself that education is about more than just numbers. Don't ignore all that standardized tests tell us, but remember, they don't define you or your students. They are just one piece of a much larger puzzle.

By keeping this perspective, you can avoid the trap of feeling like you're not doing enough. Your impact as an educator is measured in the confidence your students gain, the curiosity you ignite, and the resilience you help them build. Those are the lessons that last far beyond any test and what we really should be talking about.

19 How Can You Befriend AI?

Like it or not, artificial intelligence (AI) is here to stay—and it's already reshaping education in ways that go far beyond the latest headlines. From automated grading tools and adaptive learning platforms to the invisible algorithms shaping what students see online, AI is no longer a futuristic concept. It's quietly embedding itself into the daily rhythm of schools and into *your* daily routine.

But let's be honest: for many teachers, the reaction to this isn't excitement—it's exhaustion. It feels like just one more thing. Another shiny new tool. Another buzzword being sold as the next big revolution in education. And with workloads already overflowing, it's completely fair to ask: Can AI actually support meaningful learning? Will it protect academic integrity? What does it mean for student engagement, or for the irreplaceable role of the teacher? Now, what is the definition of plagiarism?

Or perhaps more urgently: *Can AI help lighten the load—without compromising what matters most in our classrooms?*

These aren't questions to dismiss or defer. They're exactly why teachers must be part of this conversation. AI isn't going away, but if we engage with it critically and intentionally, we have a rare opportunity to shape how it's used in our classrooms, rather than being shaped by it.

At its best, AI can function as a supportive assistant—not a replacement for your professional judgment, but a tool to help you reclaim some time and energy. It can automate the tasks that drain your focus, help differentiate instruction, offer insights into student needs, and even spark creativity when you're running on fumes. The goal isn't to replace the human heart of teaching—it's to help you preserve it.

So, how do we harness AI in a way that doesn't just make our jobs more efficient but actually helps us reconnect with the parts of teaching that brought us here in the first place—creativity, curiosity, and connection? How can we move from wary observers to thoughtful collaborators? How can we make AI our ally—maybe even our friend?

Here's one place to start: pick a task you *don't* want to do. Something that weighs you down. Maybe it's drafting an email to an upset parent. Maybe it's creating a third version of a worksheet for a student who needs extra practice. These are the moments when AI can step in and offer relief—without taking away your voice.

You already have a sense of what you want to say or what skills you want to target. So, try asking AI to help. Type in your prompt and see what it gives you. What it produces might surprise you. And in doing this, you'll probably notice three things:

First, you'll get something. Whether or not it's useful right away is another story—but you'll have a draft. A place to start. You can improve the results by being specific in your request. For example, instead of typing, "Write an email to an angry parent," try something like:

> *Please write an email to Ben's mother, Laura, who is upset that her son scored 67% on the last test. She feels the class is too hard, but Ben needs to pay more attention and ask questions when he's confused. Also, Ben has missed several classes due to hockey. I want the email to acknowledge the challenges of being a student-athlete but also communicate that I'm here to help and that Ben needs to take initiative. Please make the tone supportive but firm.*

The more context you provide, the more likely you'll get something you can work with.

Second, the first draft AI gives you doesn't have to be the last. One of AI's biggest strengths is its willingness to keep working—no eye rolls, no complaints. You can edit, refine, rephrase, and repeat until it sounds like *you*. Think of it like a conversation with a colleague: you wouldn't use their exact words, but they might help you unlock your own.

Third, you might find that what AI gives you isn't as good as what *you* would create—and that's not a bad thing. In fact, it's a powerful reminder: you have expertise, insight, and a human touch that no machine can replicate. AI might offer a starting point, but you bring the heart, the nuance, and the real understanding of your students. Sometimes, seeing what AI produces will clarify your own thinking or even inspire a better version of what you were imagining. It's not about replacing your voice—it's about helping you hear it more clearly.

Now, what about AI in the classroom? There's no shortage of advice—hundreds of books, blogs, and resources are already out there, filled with strategies, tools, and theories. You don't need to read them all. But if you're looking for inspiration or feeling stuck, many of these resources can spark ideas and help you see what's possible. Still, the most important step isn't reading—it's *trying*. Choose something small and manageable. Test it. Tweak it. Reflect on it. Whether it's a simple AI writing prompt, a student brainstorming session, or an AI-generated quiz, your willingness to explore sends a powerful message to your students: *You're paying attention. You're willing to learn. And you're modeling what it looks like to engage with technology thoughtfully.*

Just as importantly, your students need guidance. They're already encountering AI—in their apps, their homework, their daily lives. What they often lack is direction. They need to be taught how to use AI as a tool for thinking, not a shortcut around it. They need your leadership in understanding when to lean on AI, when to question it, and when to rely on their own minds. By showing them how to use AI *responsibly and creatively*, you're not just teaching content—you're teaching digital wisdom.

So, how do you befriend AI? Not by mastering every tool or becoming a tech expert overnight. You befriend it by being curious, by staying open, and by letting it serve your values—not replace them. AI doesn't need to be your enemy or your savior. It can simply be one more tool in your kit—one that helps you breathe a little easier, teach a little deeper, and lead your students with clarity and care through a rapidly changing world. Start small. Stay grounded. And remember: the most powerful technology in any classroom is still a thoughtful, empowered teacher.

20 What Does Your To-Do List Look Like?

This chapter may be the quickest and simplest to integrate into your school day—but don't let its simplicity fool you. It focuses on a tool you're already using, whether consciously or not: your To-Do list. Everyone has one. Some are neatly written on paper, some live in digital apps, and others float around in our minds. Teachers often even write them on whiteboards, not just for themselves but to keep students on track. Regardless of the format, the To-Do list is a powerful tool—when used intentionally. This chapter will show you how to refine that everyday habit to create more joy in your day and take some of the burden of feeling unproductive off your shoulders.

Before we dive into how to make your To-Do list more enjoyable, take a moment to reflect on why you make your list, what your current list looks like, and how it makes you feel. Do you make your To-Do list to feel the satisfaction of crossing tasks off once they are complete? Do you make your list to remember everything you need to do? Or is there another reason you make your lists?

What do you typically include? Are your tasks written out in quick bullet points, or do you take a more detailed, sentence-based approach? Do you jot things down first thing in the morning, or do you plan ahead the night before? Do you enjoy checking things off or just rush to the next task? Maybe your list only appears when you're feeling overwhelmed and trying to gain control. However you do it, your current system offers insight into your habits—and understanding those patterns is the first step toward creating a list that works *with* you, not against you.

Now, be honest—does your To-Do list actually help you, or does it just sit there, silently mocking you as a reminder of everything you haven't accomplished?

For many educators, the list becomes less of a productivity tool and more of a guilt trip. This is one of the biggest contributors to burnout and that creeping feeling of ineffectiveness: the frustration of consistently being unable to scratch anything off.

Take Ms. Carter, for example—a middle school science teacher in Minnesota. Every morning, she began with the best intentions and a long To-Do list: grading assignments, prepping lab materials, emailing parents, attending IEP meetings, organizing supplies ... the list never seemed to end.

By the end of each day, she felt like she'd been in constant motion, yet had somehow not crossed anything off her list. That growing, unchecked list didn't just represent unfinished tasks—it became a daily reminder that she was falling short. She was putting the right things on her list; she just didn't have the time to do them.

That feeling, day after day, made her job even harder. Now, Ms. Carter is considering leaving the profession—not because she doesn't care, but because she feels she can't do the job she *wants* to do within the time she's given. And ironically, it's her To-Do list that drives that painful truth home every single day.

The truth is, when your To-Do list becomes an ever-growing mountain rather than a set of achievable steps, it stops being helpful. We cannot create more time for ourselves, but with a few mindful adjustments, your list can shift from overwhelming to empowering—giving you not just clarity but a sense of accomplishment at the end of the day. And why not infuse some fun or relaxation into your day?

So, how can we actually start to make progress? While Ms. Carter may feel like leaving teaching is her only option, it's possible that a shift in how she approaches her To-Do list could make a meaningful difference. Sometimes, it's not about doing *more*, but about doing things *differently*. One helpful strategy is to break large, overwhelming tasks into smaller, more manageable steps. Instead of writing something big and vague like "Write mid-term comments," she could try writing just the next action: "Open laptop and write the first sentence for the first student." That small step feels doable, and once you start, it's often easier to keep going. Each tiny bit of progress builds momentum and makes the day feel more productive.

Another often-overlooked strategy is to add moments of joy to the list—on purpose. A To-Do list doesn't have to be only about productivity; it can also include things that bring lightness and recharge your energy. Items like "Take a ten-minute walk," "Call a friend," or "Enjoy a sweet treat" may seem minor, but they can provide essential mental breaks that help you stay motivated. Even something as basic as "Go to the bathroom" might need to be written down, because for many teachers, even attending to basic needs can get pushed aside during a busy day. By including small, restorative moments, the list becomes not just a task manager but a reminder to take care of yourself.

Reshaping how we interact with our To-Do lists won't solve every challenge, but it can shift our mindset from feeling constantly behind to feeling more in control. And sometimes, that shift is enough to help us keep going.

Take a moment to look at your most recent To-Do list—or if you haven't made one yet, start drafting your next one. If your lists tend to stare back at you with judgment, making you feel overwhelmed or unproductive, it might be time to rethink how you're approaching them. Try breaking larger tasks into smaller, more manageable steps. A long, vague item like "Organize next week's lesson plans" can feel impossible, but "Plan for Monday" feels doable—and checking it off builds momentum. On the other hand, if you're good at powering through your list but it feels like all work and no play, consider adding a few joyful tasks. It's okay—actually, it's *great*—to include fun on your list. Writing down something enjoyable, like "Do a crossword puzzle" or "Take a coffee break in the sun," can give you permission to slow down and recharge. Your To-Do list should help you, not haunt you—so make it something that works *with* your life, not against it.

First thing on your next To-Do list:

1 Make a To-Do lists that gets stuff done *and* makes me smile.

21 *Are You Lonely? Are Your Students Lonely?*

Vivek H. Murthy, our nineteenth and twenty-first Surgeon General of the United States, published a report in 2023 about the epidemic of loneliness in our country. It is entitled "Our Epidemic of Loneliness and Isolation" (2023). He was motivated by what he was hearing from Americans all across the nation on his cross-country listening tour. (By the way, how cool is that? He went across the country just to listen to the people he was going to serve. Nice job, Vivek!) Here is what the report said:

> In the scientific literature, I found confirmation of what I was hearing. In recent years, about one-in-two adults in America reported experiencing loneliness. And that was before the COVID-19 pandemic cut off so many of us from friends, loved ones, and support systems, exacerbating loneliness and isolation.
>
> Loneliness is far more than just a bad feeling—it harms both individual and societal health. It is associated with a greater risk of cardiovascular disease, dementia, stroke, depression, anxiety, and premature death. The mortality impact of being socially disconnected is similar to that caused by smoking up to 15 cigarettes a day, and even greater than that associated with obesity and physical inactivity. And the harmful consequences of a society that lacks social connection can be felt in our schools, workplaces, and civic organizations, where performance, productivity, and engagement are diminished.[1]

That is quite a staggering statement, isn't it? Take a moment now to pause and reflect—Are you feeling lonely? Are your students lonely? How do you know if you suffer from loneliness? Think about these questions: Do you wish you had more people in your life that you deeply connected with? Do you feel isolated—even in a crowd? Do you doubt your worth? Do you feel empty, or do you feel like something is missing in your life?

According to the data, there's a strong possibility that you—and some of your students—are experiencing loneliness. If that is the case, I want to say sincerely: I am truly sorry. Loneliness is most definitely a symptom of burnout.

One of the most difficult aspects of loneliness is the shame that often surrounds it. Many people feel embarrassed to admit they are lonely, as if loneliness itself is a personal failure. This shame traps individuals in silence, making it even harder to seek the support and connection they desperately need. It reinforces the harmful idea that struggles must be borne alone.

As a society, we tend to overvalue independence, celebrating self-sufficiency as a marker of strength and success. While autonomy is important, this cultural emphasis often comes at the expense of recognizing our fundamental need for connection. We forget that humans are inherently social creatures, made to live in community. From an evolutionary standpoint, our survival depended on collaboration—on tribes, families, and shared resources. But this isn't just history; it's embedded in our biology.

Our brains are literally wired for connection. The human nervous system is built to attune to others. When we engage in meaningful social interaction, our brains release oxytocin, sometimes called the "bonding hormone," which fosters trust and closeness. Mirror neurons allow us to empathize and read each other's emotions. Neural networks in the brain's default mode are most active when we are thinking about ourselves in relation to others—our relationships, our place in the world, and how we are perceived.

Despite this wiring, modern society often leads us to believe that we should face our challenges alone. We are told to "tough it out," to "figure it out" on our own. As a result, we may come to believe that our struggles are uniquely ours—that no one else could possibly understand what we are going through. This mindset doesn't empower us; it isolates us. It silences us. And that isolation can trigger stress responses in the brain—elevating cortisol levels and reinforcing the sense of being unsafe, unseen, and disconnected.

What we often need most isn't advice or solutions, but presence—someone to sit with us, to affirm that we're not alone. Healing happens in relationship.

Growth is nurtured in community. When we lean into connection rather than away from it, we align with the way our brains—and our hearts—are made to function.

The path to true community begins not with perfection or performance but with honesty. When we allow ourselves to be vulnerable—naming our struggles instead of concealing them—we create space for authentic connection. Vulnerability is not weakness; it's an invitation. It signals to others that they are not alone, and it opens the door for mutual support and understanding. In sharing our burdens, we don't add weight to others—we lighten the collective load. We step into our shared humanity, where healing and belonging can begin to take root.

When loneliness is hidden, it becomes an invisible burden, growing heavier over time. But when we recognize this reality, we open the door to change. We create space for openness, compassion, and meaningful relationships to take root and thrive. This is exactly what the Surgeon General's report says we need to do in our schools, "develop social skills and strengthen relationships."[2] All of us, not just our students. We are never too old to develop stronger social skills.

So how do we do this? First, we must admit that we have helped in creating the problem. Think about your home. Do you know your neighbors? Do you try to build a sense of community where you live? For many people, the answer is no. We've grown attached to our privacy—sometimes to the point of isolation. As home delivery becomes the norm, and as digital conveniences allow us to avoid face-to-face interactions, the opportunities for spontaneous connection are disappearing. We've traded social effort for comfort and efficiency. But this trade-off has a price: increasing loneliness. In our quest to be left alone, we may be forgetting how to truly connect, and we underestimate how much we need these connections.

Do we fall into the same patterns at work? Absolutely. It's often easier to send an email than to walk down the hall and have a real conversation. We hide behind screens, tucked away in our classrooms or offices, avoiding the effort—and vulnerability—of human interaction. When someone asks how we're doing, we default to "I'm fine," even when we're not. We avoid eye contact in meetings, opt out of social gatherings, and convince ourselves that staying busy is the same as staying connected. But it's not. These small acts of social avoidance add up. They create workplaces full of isolated individuals who feel unseen and unheard. If we're not careful, the workplace becomes just another space where loneliness can thrive, masked by productivity and convenience and leading to more burnout.

Now, I'm not saying you need to make work your entire social life, but you do need to build genuine personal connections at work in order to thrive and be the teacher you want to be. These relationships don't just make the workplace more enjoyable—they help prevent burnout by creating a sense of support, belonging, and shared purpose. When we feel seen and valued, we're more resilient, more engaged, and far less likely to feel overwhelmed or alone.

22 How Can You Create a United Front with Parents and Guardians?

Working with parents and guardians is a crucial aspect of your role as a teacher, and it can be a rewarding experience, though not always easy. Sometimes the conversations go smoothly, but other times they can be challenging, to say the least. One of the best pieces of advice I've received is to simply listen. Often, when parents reach out, they're feeling overwhelmed—angry, confused, or frustrated—and what they truly need is someone who will listen without judgment. In many cases, offering a listening ear can be more valuable than immediately jumping to a solution. Just being heard can help them feel understood and supported.

Listening is the foundation of any strong relationship, and this holds especially true in the partnership between educators and families. When you take the time to truly listen to parents or guardians, you demonstrate respect, understanding, and a shared commitment to the student's success. This not only builds trust but also fosters open communication, making it easier to work together effectively.

By presenting a united front, you and the student's family create a consistent and supportive environment that encourages growth. When students see that the adults in their lives are aligned in their expectations and approach, they are less likely to manipulate situations or create divides. Instead, they come to understand that their success is a collective goal, supported by both home and school.

Good listening skills on your part help make this possible. When parents feel heard and valued, they are more likely to collaborate with you, reinforcing positive messages and strategies at home. This alignment creates a seamless support system, ensuring that the student receives consistent guidance, accountability, and encouragement both in and out of the classroom.

My mom once shared with me a powerful idea she had about the importance of listening. She wanted to start a service where people could come in, and she would simply sit with them, listen, and offer a space for them to be heard. She wouldn't say anything—she would just listen. She believed that, sometimes, just being listened to—without advice or judgment—was enough to help people feel validated and ready to move forward. She even reached out to her local library to explore the idea of renting a room there and offering her services, but, unfortunately, it never came to fruition. Still, I can't help but think that one day, it could become a reality.

My mom's belief in the power of listening has helped me over the years. I have had upset and emotional parents on the phone or in my classroom more times than I can count. Once I realized that listening to them was the best thing I could do, everything went better than expected. Even if they ask me questions or want my advice, I got good at saying, "Well, what do you think?" or "What do you think will best support your child?" Now, there are times that I do have information that I need to share, but I only do so once I have given the parents or guardians a chance to talk and a chance to be heard.

Once you've ensured that the parent feels heard and understood, you can begin discussing next steps. Ask, "What can *we* do to better support your child?" Clearly outlining action steps is an effective way to conclude the meeting. Be specific about what each person will do to help support the child and their family.

One key point to remember: after the meeting, always follow up with the parent as soon as possible. Parents need reassurance that both their child's well-being and their concerns are being taken seriously. Even if there's no significant update to share, a brief check-in—whether by phone or email—within a week can make a world of difference. It shows the parent you are committed to their child's success and that they're not facing challenges alone.

Another key benefit of actively engaging with parents is the wealth of insights it provides—not only about their child but also about the broader community's perspectives and attitudes toward the school. Parents often share their thoughts and experiences with one another, offering valuable feedback that can help educators and administrators better understand the needs and concerns of the community. Strong communication between parents and guardians can transform a good school into an exceptional one, fostering a more supportive and collaborative environment for everyone involved.

When parents and guardians are working with you as partners, rather than against you, it reduces stress and builds a collaborative support network for the student. This fosters a sense of community and strengthens the support system around the child. Creating a positive and supportive environment benefits everyone, and I assure you, it will make your job not only easier but also more fulfilling. When you invest in clear communication, collaboration, and thoughtful interactions, you'll find that challenges become more manageable, relationships strengthen, and daily tasks feel less overwhelming. The effort you put in now will pay off in ways you might not even expect.

23 What Are the Lingering Effects from COVID in Your Students?

We can all agree that COVID had a profound impact on everyone, but the full extent of its lingering effects may be more significant than we initially realized. Consider the kids in your classroom—if these are high school students, many of them were in elementary school or younger when the pandemic struck. This was a critical time for their social, emotional, and cognitive development. The isolation they experienced during those formative years is bound to have lasting consequences. How are those early disruptions shaping their interactions, their emotional well-being, and their ability to navigate the world today?

I am well aware of the academic and cognitive setbacks caused by the pandemic. While I wish our school had done more to address those losses, it's not worth dwelling on what could have been done differently now. What I hadn't fully considered, however, is the emotional toll. Let me explain. A respected English teacher I know recently expressed his concern about the lack of emotional responses he's observing in his students when they engage with tragic or emotionally charged literature. He noted that their emotional intelligence appears to be noticeably lower than it once was, leaving him puzzled. Emotions like sadness, fear, desperation, and hopelessness seem to be met with indifference, and empathy for the characters is often absent as well. This shift is something he's struggling to understand.

Once he pointed it out, I began noticing it more than I had before. It could be a lingering effect of COVID, or perhaps it's the constant access to phones and social media that fills every spare moment. Whatever the cause, I can't help but feel that my students seem more emotionally immature than I remember. I would love to see schools talking about this. What can we do to help our students become more empathetic, aware, and emotionally available to each other? How can we better listen to each other and help others feel seen and heard? Let's not limit this to our students. How can we do this for each other too?

My hope is that once the conversation begins, we will all engage in more meaningful dialogue and truly listen to one another. Teachers can lead the way by modeling this behavior for students. We can each take the time to nurture our emotional well-being, especially in a time when loneliness has become a silent pandemic in our society. By making small but significant changes, we can be the change we wish to see in the world, starting within the walls of our schools.

This is not intended to be yet another responsibility added to teachers' already full plates. Instead, it should be something that teachers embrace for their own well-being first and then extend to their students. It's about enriching the time we spend together—creating moments to honor one another, to truly see, listen to, and care for each other. Teachers, at their core, long to create these connections, and this is an opportunity for all of us to bring that vision to life.

How do we do this? David Brooks, in his book *How to Know a Person: The Art of Seeing Others Deeply and Being Seen Deeply*, says that we are falling short in our schools because we do not teach these skills. He says,

> *In this age of creeping dehumanization, I've become obsessed with social skills: how to get better at treating people with consideration; how to get better at understanding the people right around us. I've come to believe that the quality of our lives and the health of our society depends, to a large degree, on how well we treat each other in the minute interactions of daily life.*[1]

To do this, Brooks says that we need "the ability to understand what another person is going through … to accurately know another person, to let them feel valued, heard and understood."[2] Let's do that for our students. Let's do that for each other.

Whether this decline in emotional maturity stems from the lasting effects of COVID, the pervasive influence of social media, or the increasing demands placed on faculty, the reality remains the same—we must navigate the consequences. While we may not be able to change these larger societal forces overnight, we can start by focusing on the small, everyday interactions that shape our school environment.

One manageable and meaningful step is to approach our interactions with greater empathy and awareness. Taking the time to truly listen, acknowledge the struggles of others, and offer support when needed can foster a more understanding and compassionate school community. By being intentional in how we communicate and engage with one another, we create a culture where emotional growth is nurtured rather than stunted. Change may not happen immediately, but small, consistent efforts can lead to a stronger, more emotionally resilient community and classroom.

24 Why Is Uncle Bob So Smart?

Every so often, someone says something that helps you more than you ever could have imagined—something that sticks, reshapes your thinking, and quietly guides you in the moments you need it most. For me, that someone was my brother-in-law, Bob. Or, as we lovingly call him, *Uncle Bob*.

Uncle Bob once shared a story with me about a frustrating period at work. His employees kept coming to him, overwhelmed and discouraged, listing all the things they couldn't do. *This client is too demanding. That schedule never works. This system is impossible to implement.* The list went on and on. Uncle Bob would patiently listen, nodding as they vented—but then, when they finished, he would offer a calm but firm response: "I hear you. But now I want you to answer one question. What *can* you do?"

That was it. One simple question—but it shifted the entire energy of the conversation. It moved people from a place of helplessness to a place of agency. It was like flipping a light switch, transforming defeat into determination. That question—*What can you do?*—has echoed in my mind ever since. It's not just smart business strategy; it's a mindset (a growth mindset)—a forward-thinking approach to problem-solving, and, honestly, a little bit of magic.

As educators, we often face our own version of this challenge. There's nothing that takes the wind out of your sails quite like a student saying, "I'm so lost—I need you to reteach me *everything*." That kind of statement can feel overwhelming, even paralyzing. But in those moments, I think of Uncle Bob. I remind myself to acknowledge the frustration, yes—but not to get stuck there. Before diving into a full reteach, I gently ask the student, "Okay—but first, tell me, what *can* you do?" As students slowly respond, they see that they know more than they thought. With a little encouragement, you can help them *discover* how much they already know, rather than you simply *telling* them. You can sit with them in their frustration and confusion and help guide them. But remember, they are doing the work—not you. They are digging deep because you asked them to show you what they can do. They are going to produce the work, and you are going to wait for them to show you something—anything that they can build upon with your guidance, and then ultimately, on their own.

And here's the hard truth: When we step in and carry the weight of someone else's challenges, even with the best intentions, we can unintentionally rob them of the opportunity to grow through their struggles. We absorb their stress, we repeat lessons they've already encountered, and we apologize for their missteps before they've had the chance to truly learn from them. In doing so, we not only exhaust ourselves—we also keep them from developing the resilience and independence they need. In this moment, it may feel like you are not doing enough, but that is far from the truth. This is where the real work lies: resisting the urge to step in and instead allowing your students to rise to the challenge. Let them do the work. Let them grow.

This cycle can quietly drain us, becoming a hidden source of burnout more than we often realize. As educators, being helpful feels like second nature—it's wired into who we are. But it's worth pausing to consider: What does truly helpful support look like?

Sometimes, in our eagerness to assist, we cross the line from supporting into rescuing and enabling. And while that might offer a quick fix, it can rob our students of the very discomfort that teaches the most. Growth isn't always graceful, and learning doesn't always feel good in the moment. But letting them wrestle with the challenge, sit in the struggle, and work through the discomfort is not neglect—it's empowerment. Resisting the urge to step in and fix everything for your students not only preserves your energy—it also protects you from the kind of emotional exhaustion that comes from constantly carrying someone else's load. Support doesn't mean carrying them. It means walking beside them, guiding when needed, and trusting them to do the hard work of learning. By allowing students to do the heavy lifting themselves, you give them the chance to grow—and give yourself the space to sustain your passion for teaching.

So … why is Uncle Bob so smart? Maybe it's because he knew that the right question, asked at the right moment, can change everything. Maybe he's a really good manager. Or maybe—just maybe—he's a magician.

25 *What Are Your Non-Negotiables?*

You may recall that, earlier in this book, you were invited to reflect on your quintessential questions—the ones that guide your teaching, shape your values, motivate your thinking, and help you grow as an educator. These are the questions that push you to refine your craft and stay connected to your purpose. Now, it's time to dig deeper. I invite you to consider another foundational element of your teaching philosophy: your non-negotiables. What are the core principles, practices, or beliefs you refuse to compromise on, no matter the circumstance? These non-negotiables serve as your compass in the classroom and beyond, grounding your decisions and sustaining your integrity in the face of challenges.

Let me share one of my own non-negotiables with you. In every aspect of my work—whether I'm planning a lesson, managing a classroom issue, contributing to a committee, or designing curriculum—I consistently return to one guiding question: "Is this the best decision for students?" This simple yet powerful question keeps me grounded and aligned with my core purpose as an educator. It helps me navigate difficult choices, especially when the easier or more convenient option presents itself. While it's often tempting to choose the path of least resistance or avoid controversy, I've learned that doing what is truly best for students is always the most responsible—and rewarding—choice.

Of course, I don't claim to have all the answers or to hold a monopoly on what's best for students. Education is far too complex and dynamic for any one person to make those decisions in isolation. What matters most is the willingness to ask the question—and to keep asking it. Engaging in thoughtful dialogue with colleagues, listening to diverse perspectives, and collectively working toward student-centered solutions is not only wise, it's essential. The best outcomes often emerge through collaboration, where shared values and open conversations guide us. And at the heart of every meaningful debate or discussion, one guiding principle should remain constant: *What is best for students?* That question must always stay at the center—it's our true north.

Sometimes, staying focused on what's best for students is more challenging than it appears. Take a topic like the dress code—something seemingly straightforward that can quickly ignite a passionate debate. Everyone brings their own perspectives, values, and experiences to the table, and rarely are two opinions exactly alike. Yet, despite the differing viewpoints, the goal remains the same: a policy that genuinely supports students and their learning. But that raises a critical question—*what does that actually mean?* What does it look like for a dress code to serve students well? Every school says they have a dress code, but *why* do they have a dress code? This is where the real work begins: listening deeply, reflecting honestly, and keeping student needs at the center of the conversation.

And if you were hoping I'd offer the perfect solution to the dress code debate, I'm afraid I'll have to disappoint you—I don't have one. The only thing I can say with certainty is this: Whatever your policy is, enforce it consistently. Students and teachers deserve clarity, fairness, and follow-through.

A second non-negotiable for me is never appearing too busy—both in reality and in perception. It's important that students and colleagues not only *can* reach out but also *feel comfortable* doing so. I make a conscious effort to stay present, approachable, and responsive. As someone who has felt intimidated by busy people, I work hard to avoid projecting that image myself. If I seem unapproachable or overwhelmed, I risk missing meaningful connections and opportunities to help—and that's not acceptable to me. Staying visibly available is a core value I actively protect.

When I asked teachers what their non-negotiables were, it turned out to be a powerful and eye-opening exercise. At first, many responded by saying they had never considered the question before. However, once they began to think it through, they were able to articulate clear, thoughtful, and often deeply personal responses. These conversations revealed not only what they value most in their classrooms—such as respect, consistency, or student engagement—but also highlighted the passion and intentionality behind their teaching practices. It's been a meaningful way to surface core beliefs and foster deeper dialogue around what truly matters in education. I felt genuinely honored that they trusted me enough to share such meaningful insights into their beliefs and values.

Here are a few responses that stood out, both deep and practical:

- *"I always go to the restroom when I need to."*
- *"I never let disrespectful behavior escalate in my classroom. If it happens, I try to stop it immediately, and if possible, talk about it with the entire class."*
- *"I don't do schoolwork at home over the weekend."*
- *"I try very hard not to say anything a student can say. I want them to be as much of the lesson as possible. This means, letting them explain information and ask questions. I want my lessons to have less of me and more of them."*
- *"I don't let a bad day ruin my evening. I make peace with the day before I go home."*
- *"I stay out of the faculty room. I don't need to be around teachers whose bitterness is getting the best of them."*
- *"I never speak negatively about a student. While I may express concerns about specific behaviors, I avoid publicly criticizing any individual student."*

Even if you haven't explicitly stated them, I'm confident there are certain non-negotiables in your teaching practice—core values or boundaries you hold firmly. What are the aspects of your work that you are absolutely not willing to compromise on, no matter the circumstance?

Sometimes, when your non-negotiables are constantly tested or undermined, it doesn't just create frustration—it can lead to real burnout. You get exhausted from fighting the same battles over and over, defending the core values or boundaries that should never have been in question in the first place.

So, what can you do when your non-negotiables are under threat? The hard truth is, sometimes the healthiest option is to walk away—to find another job, another environment, another place that respects what matters most to you. But what if leaving isn't immediately possible?

In those moments, protecting your peace becomes critical. That might mean setting firmer boundaries, finding allies who share your values, or redefining how much energy you're willing to give to a system that doesn't align with your principles. It might also involve therapy, mindfulness practices, or simply giving yourself permission to disengage emotionally from situations that drain you.

Your well-being is not negotiable. If the system around you refuses to respect your limits, then you have to be the one to reinforce them—for your own sanity, your own health, and your future.

The good news is, reclaiming your non-negotiables can be empowering. Re-centering your values—even in small, daily ways—can reignite your purpose and remind you why you chose this work in the first place. You deserve to feel grounded, respected, and fulfilled in your role. So, take a moment to name your non-negotiables, protect them fiercely, and know that doing so isn't selfish—it's essential. When you honor what matters most to you, you create a teaching life that's not just sustainable but deeply rewarding—and perhaps, little by little, burnout begins to fade.

26 *Are You a Giver or a Taker? Wait—You're a Teacher, So You're a Giver*

My dad used to say there are two kinds of people in the world: givers and takers. He not only urged us kids to be givers but also lived that principle every day through his generosity and willingness to help others as a military officer and a therapist. As teachers, I think we are, by design, all givers. This is a wonderful part of the job, but it is in this very nature that we can sometimes find our greatest vulnerability. Givers often pour themselves out for others—offering time, energy, and emotional support far beyond what is required. And while the rewards of giving are real and meaningful, there is a hidden cost if we are not careful: the slow creep of exhaustion, depletion, and ultimately burnout.

This advice has also been a steady anchor for me during times when I found myself struggling with a student, a colleague, or even a friend. Whenever I asked myself, *Why is this relationship so hard? Why do I feel so drained?* I often discovered the same answer: More times than not, it was because I was the giver—and they were the taker. That realization hit hard. It wasn't that they were bad people or that I resented them; it was that I hadn't recognized the imbalance that was slowly exhausting me. My father's wisdom helped me understand that while being a giver is a strength, it also makes you vulnerable to relationships where the flow of energy is one-sided. When the giving flows only in one direction, it becomes less an act of kindness and more an act of depletion. Recognizing this pattern gave me the clarity to set better boundaries and protect my own well-being while still staying true to the values my father taught me.

The truth is, even the most generous well can run dry. When we give without boundaries, we risk emptying ourselves to the point where we can no longer serve anyone well—not our students, not our colleagues, and certainly not ourselves. The danger is not in the act of giving itself, but in giving without recognizing our own limits. We must remember that sustainability matters; we cannot light the path for others if our own flame has burned out.

Learning to balance generosity with self-preservation is one of the hardest—and most important—lessons for any giver—and teacher. It means recognizing when to say no, when to step back, and when to replenish our own reserves. It means allowing ourselves the same care, compassion, and patience we so readily offer to others. Being a giver is indeed a beautiful way to move through the world—but only if we remember that we, too, are worthy of receiving.

You've heard this all before, but it bears repeating: as a natural giver, you must learn to manage your generosity if you want to sustain it over the long haul. It's easy to fall into the trap of thinking you can—or should—give endlessly, but even the most generous heart has limits. One of the first and most important steps is setting clear boundaries. Saying no is not selfish; it is an act of wisdom and care. Without limits, you risk stretching yourself so thin that you can no longer offer meaningful help to anyone. Boundaries help protect your energy so you can give intentionally, not reactively.

Another essential practice is scheduling time for yourself. This is not an indulgence; it's a necessity. Whether it's blocking out a quiet hour to recharge, pursuing a hobby, or simply stepping away from work for a real break, you need space that is just yours. (I would even encourage you to do this at work—daily.)

Alongside this, remember that you don't have to carry everything alone. Ask for help when you need it. Too often, givers hesitate to become receivers, but letting others support you strengthens your capacity and reminds you that you are part of a larger, shared effort. Asking for help isn't a natural tendency for givers. You will need to work on this.

Regular self-check-ins are equally important. Pause often to ask yourself how you're really doing. Are you feeling tired, resentful, overwhelmed? These are warning lights on the dashboard of your well-being, telling you it's time to adjust. They are also indicators of burnout. Don't ignore them. And when you catch yourself trying to over-deliver or perfect every task, practice reminding yourself that "enough" truly is enough. Not every lesson, meeting, or moment has to be flawless.

Finally, reconnect with your "why." Remind yourself what called you to this path in the first place. When you focus on what truly matters, you can make better decisions about where to direct your limited energy and time. Remember, managing your giving nature isn't about giving less—it's about giving wisely, so your generosity can last. You are not a limitless well, and that's okay. By caring for yourself, you preserve the very heart that allows you to care for others. Please guard that beautiful and giving heart of yours!

27 Why Will Neuroscience Never Let You Down?

If you've been in education for any length of time, you've likely witnessed a wide array of pedagogical trends rise to prominence—each promising to revolutionize teaching and learning. From Differentiated Instruction to Investigative Learning, from Competency-Based Education to Project-Based Learning, the landscape of educational theory is constantly evolving. We've seen Open Classrooms, Virtual Classrooms, and Flipped Classrooms—all aiming to reshape the way students engage with content and with each other. And still, there is more, and the list continues to grow.

Each of these approaches brings its own strengths and challenges. Some emphasize student autonomy, while others focus on mastery of core competencies or the importance of real-world application. As educators, we find ourselves adapting, experimenting, and sometimes even cycling back to familiar practices with a new lens.

While the terminology may shift and the methods may vary, the goal remains the same: to engage students in meaningful learning experiences that foster growth, understanding, and a lifelong love of learning. The real art lies in weaving these evolving ideas into practice in a way that aligns with our unique teaching styles and personalities, while thoughtfully addressing the diverse needs of our students, classrooms, and communities.

But navigating this ever-changing landscape isn't always easy. It can be overwhelming—and at times, downright confusing and frustrating. Where is our true north? What truths can we confidently hold onto? In a sea of shifting paradigms, what remains steady and reliable? The pedagogical landscape is a bit like New England weather: if you don't like the current trend, just wait a few minutes—something new is bound to blow in.

One powerful way to feel more grounded and productive is to turn to *educational neuroscience*—a growing field that brings together neuroscience, pedagogy, and psychology. We're fortunate to live in a time when we can observe the brain in action as it thinks and learns. This allows us to explore how learning happens at a biological level, helping us improve educational outcomes.

Educational neuroscience seeks to bridge the gap between research and practice, offering evidence-based strategies and tools that benefit both teachers and students. As one researcher put it, "We are the first generation to develop a deep understanding of how the brain learns, works, changes, and thrives. Yet schools have changed so little as a result of this work."[1]

But there's no need to feel overwhelmed. The field of neuroscience is vast, and there are plenty of accessible resources—books, conferences, and journals—that can support your journey. Better yet, you don't need to overhaul everything at once. Small, actionable strategies can make a big difference. You want to take what the brain research is showing us about learning and bring that into the classroom. Remember, as teachers, we are "brain changers."[2]

So, what can you do? Here is one idea: try limiting the matching section of your assessments to just four to seven items, ensuring each column is concise, clear, and logically organized. This simple adjustment can help reduce the cognitive load. Additionally, the brain learns more effectively when information is grouped into meaningful "chunks." Organizing material by theme or topic can enhance retention. And don't underestimate the power of environment—since the brain is highly susceptible to distraction, creating a calm, quiet space is more essential for optimal learning than we may have realized.

One significant finding from recent brain research that is worth mentioning is the debunking of the traditional concept of "learning styles." The idea that individuals learn best through a specific modality—such as visual, auditory, or kinesthetic—has not held up under scientific scrutiny. In fact, clinging to this belief can create a fixed mindset in students, limiting their potential. When students identify themselves as only visual learners or insist that they can only understand material when it's read aloud to them, they inadvertently restrict their own learning possibilities. This mindset can hinder academic growth and reduce adaptability. In reality, the brain is highly flexible, and effective learning often involves engaging multiple senses and strategies. It's more beneficial to help students recognize that they have access to a diverse set of cognitive tools. The real skill lies in teaching them how to strategically select and apply these tools based on the task at hand. Encouraging this flexible, metacognitive approach fosters resilience, independence, and a deeper understanding of how learning works.

Consider this: Research consistently shows that when teachers deepen their understanding of how the brain learns, it leads to increased instructional effectiveness, greater teacher confidence, and improved student outcomes. Despite this, most educator preparation programs and school-based professional development opportunities still do not require a foundational knowledge of brain-based learning. This gap may be one of the greatest ironies in education—How can we teach effectively without understanding how learning actually happens? For many educators, this knowledge may not have been part of their formal training. If that's the case, you may need to take the initiative to seek out this understanding yourself—but the effort is well worth it, with the potential to transform both your teaching and your students' learning.

So, let's summarize: In a world of ever-evolving educational trends and shifting teaching philosophies, neuroscience offers a steady and empowering foundation. This chapter reminds us that amid the whirlwind of pedagogical buzzwords and classroom reinventions, the most enduring truth lies in understanding how the brain learns. Educational neuroscience bridges the gap between research and practice, offering practical, brain-friendly strategies that can be easily woven into any teaching style. With simple, science-backed adjustments—like reducing cognitive load and fostering metacognitive thinking—educators can make a powerful impact without overhauling their entire approach. Most importantly, it calls on teachers to embrace their roles as "brain changers," equipped with the remarkable opportunity to shape not just what students learn, but how they grow as learners. In this light, neuroscience isn't just a tool—it's a hopeful, reliable guide in the journey of education.

28 *You Are Going to Have Problems. What Kind of Problems Do You Want?*

It's a strange and unfortunate reality in the world of education that so many teachers equate "moving up" or earning a promotion with leaving the classroom for administration. Why have we come to accept this as the main path for career advancement? Of course, for those who genuinely want to shape school-wide decisions, influence policies, or manage broader systems, stepping into an administrative role makes sense. But let's be honest—How many passionate educators *really* want to give up the daily, meaningful work of interacting with students? Why is it that in a profession centered on student learning and growth, the only recognized form of professional advancement often requires stepping away from the very heart of that work? And let's state the obvious: Anyone who aspires to lead schools without first spending time in the classroom misses a crucial part of the foundation needed to truly understand and support teaching and learning.

What if we reimagined career pathways for teachers—pathways that reward mastery, innovation, and leadership *within* the classroom rather than outside of it? What if we valued expert teachers not just as instructors, but as mentors, curriculum designers, instructional leaders, and catalysts for change, without forcing them to leave the students they inspire every day? It's time to rethink what progress and promotion mean in education and to build systems that let teachers grow while staying connected to the work they love most. Perhaps what we need isn't more administrative positions but more empowered and valued teachers whose voices help shape the direction of schools. But that conversation and brainstorming session is for another day.

Let's focus on you. You may have aspirations of becoming an administrator—and those aspirations might be grounded in all the right reasons. Maybe you want to shape school culture, support teachers, or help create more equitable systems. These are noble and necessary goals. But before making the leap out of the classroom, it's important to pause and reflect on what kind of work—and what kind of challenges—will begin to occupy your days.

One of the biggest shifts is this: The nature of your relationships changes. As a classroom teacher, your primary focus is on students—forming meaningful connections, supporting their growth, and witnessing their daily progress. Once you step into an administrative role, however, your work becomes centered around adults. You'll be navigating staff dynamics, managing team morale, addressing conflicts, and often handling complex issues that stretch beyond the professional into the personal.

This kind of leadership can be deeply rewarding—but it can also be unexpectedly isolating. The close-knit community you create in your classroom, where trust and shared purpose grow naturally over time, is not easily replicated at the leadership level. Building trust with adults, especially in a supervisory role, is harder, slower, and often more politically fraught. Some of the joy you once found in your daily work—the small victories with students, the spontaneous moments of connection—can feel more distant in an office down the hall.

And then there's the emotional toll—one that's often underestimated. As a teacher, you work closely with students who are still growing, still forming their identities, and often more open to guidance and change. There's a sense of hope in that work, a feeling that your influence can truly shape a young life. But when you become an administrator, the focus shifts to adults—colleagues who may be set in their ways, carrying years of unspoken frustrations, personal stress, or burnout. Supporting teachers through professional struggles, personal crises, or emotional exhaustion requires a different kind of emotional bandwidth—one that many don't anticipate. And unlike the classroom, where small wins are visible and frequent, the rewards in leadership can feel distant and delayed. Add to that the reality that administrators often lack the same support systems they once relied on as teachers, and it's no surprise that many find themselves feeling isolated—carrying the weight of others' burdens with few places to set down their own.

So, if you're considering this move, do it with clear eyes and honest reflection. Don't just ask yourself *why* you want to lead—ask *who* you want to serve and *how* you're prepared to serve them. Are you ready for the profound shift in relationships, responsibilities, and daily purpose that comes with stepping away from the classroom? Challenges will come either way—the question is, what kind of challenges are you willing to face every day? Choose the problems that align with your values and the kind of impact you truly want to make.

29 So, What Do the Experts Say?

Jenny Farmelo is a Christian Life Coach who specializes in helping individuals navigate the challenges of burnout. Her goal is equipping and empowering people to live their most abundant lives. While therapy often focuses on unpacking the past, life coaching is about moving forward with intention. Jenny's approach is rooted in optimism and empowerment. She calls herself a strategic encourager while guiding her clients to ask themselves, "How do I want to show up?" *and* "Who do I want to be now?" These powerful questions shift the focus to the present, encouraging individuals to take ownership of their lives and well-being—without waiting for their circumstances to change.

Jenny teaches that our thoughts and emotions play a significant role in shaping our experiences. By becoming more aware of our mental patterns, we can learn to manage our minds rather than be controlled by negative thoughts or overwhelming emotions. She encourages her clients to embrace the process of *thinking, feeling, and choosing*—a framework that helps individuals cultivate awareness, make intentional choices, and ultimately shape how they show up in their daily lives. The key is recognizing what you need and making conscious adjustments to support your mental and emotional health, or as Jenny says, "Pursue wholeness in mind, body and spirit."

This is a practiced skill that can be learned. First, becoming aware of what you are actually thinking, feeling, and choosing. This is done through a lens of compassion and curiosity. This might also require you to tune into your feelings and learn how to process them in a healthy way. Secondly, deciding if this is what you want to continue to think about, feel, or choose. It might be helpful to ask yourself, "What am I creating here?"

If the results are not what you want, you can learn to change your perspective. It is incredibly empowering to recognize that you can have agency over your thoughts, feelings, and actions. This helps you move from feeling like a victim in your circumstances to the hero or heroine of your story. This will involve making intentional choices about how you want to support yourself. This might include making sure you are creating rhythms of rest, recreation, connection, and creativity. When you build these into your everyday life, you will show up differently. What a wonderful prospective Jenny offers us.

Michelle Barrett, a practicing psychologist, college professor and high school AP Psycholgy teacher, is a passionate advocate for the practice of self-care—not only as a means of maintaining personal well-being but also as a powerful tool for influencing the culture around us. She often emphasizes that when educators prioritize their own health and balance, they send a clear and impactful message to students and colleagues: self-care is not indulgent—it's essential. Read how encouraging and insightful she is:

I am a licensed clinical psychologist and former professor of psychology who taught undergraduate, masters, and doctoral courses for 20 plus years. I loved teaching college—doing research, being an expert in my field, and helping students prepare for a career in psychology. When I left academia, I planned to focus solely on my clinical practice which has always been an important part of my life and career. During COVID I was asked to teach AP Psychology in a high school and for the last 5 years have taught five sections of AP Psychology to juniors and seniors. Two things became immediately clear to me—I have never worked harder and I have never had more fun in my job.

If I'm honest, the first thing I noticed was that I felt trapped by the everyday 7:45am–3:45pm routine. The pace of the day is insane, there are no real breaks, and taking a day off, even when sick, is often more trouble than it's worth. A mentor of mine who was a psychologist and professor told me that teaching is much harder than doing therapy because you are not dealing with one personality across from you, but instead you are managing and being present to MANY personalities at the same time and that can be exhausting.

Throughout my career, I did many in-service presentations to K-12 teachers. I quickly learned that they could be a tough crowd and the worst thing you could do was waste their time! Teachers are masters at planning, structure, and efficiency in their own classrooms, so don't show up unprepared or with material that is meaningless and irrelevant to what they do every day. Don't waste their time with what could have been an email. Don't add another thing to their plate, micro-manage them, or tell them things they already know.

I always enjoyed teaching, but there was something special about the energy of high school students that ended up giving me energy. I remember a moment at end of my first semester teaching high school; we had some time at the end of class and a student asked if she could play holiday music. Before I knew it the students were singing and dancing and having so much fun. I can only describe it as joyful. I decided that this is where I needed to be and slowly began to give myself permission to have more fun with my students.

So, I try to bring joyful play into my class each day. Play is the language of childhood—it's how very young kids learn to communicate and be social. I think that all ages need play including adults. Let me be clear that I am strict about mutual respect in the classroom. I show up with energy to teach and while I'm teaching, I expect their full attention or the very best they can do that day. I love that teachers bring their unique styles, personalities, hobbies and passions to the classroom. While I'm sure that our students remember certain facts, vocabulary, and formulas, I'm convinced that they really remember our stories, kindness, humor, and the way that we made them feel seen and valued.

Everyone is different, but for me I try to make my classroom environment welcoming—imagining that this is OUR home for at least a while. For me that means a candle burning with a candle warmer, having blankets around the room for coziness, and greeting each student by name with a smile. Sometimes, while taking attendance, I ask the students to talk to their neighbor for 2 minutes about some topic I offer (cereal with milk or without) or how they are doing. Sometimes I have students take turns playing a song of the day (I learned it's important to clarify clean versions only!), or we might do a few jumping jacks, have a mini dance party, or take a few deep breaths together. Just a few minutes of class time can shift the energy of the room and allow students some playtime before they shift into student mode. And if possible, I try to end the class with a few minutes for themselves—putting their head down to rest, socializing, listening to music on AirPods or even checking their phones!

Reducing anxiety in the room is a big part of what I try to do. I do this through how I teach, how I speak to students and most importantly, how I assess their understanding. I believe in transparent testing—I tell them what I want them to know and what to study—no surprises. I've spent 20 plus years working with individuals with test anxiety, so I get that this is a real thing. Many tests are structured to raise student anxiety where I prefer to lower anxiety and allow students to show up prepared. This is something I did in college courses as well. In my experience students studied more and reported scoring higher on my exams than others in their lives. Many times, students told me it was the first time they felt smart.

Psychology is a subject that has so much applicability to life so creating enjoyable activities is easy. One of my favorites is the sleep lab. AP Psychology curriculum covers the biology, stages, and importance of sleep. Once we learn this material the students have a sleep lab. They find a comfy spot on the floor or just resting their heads on the desk. I do a guided relaxation script and they go to sleep (or rest). It's one of the favorite things we do all year.

All teachers have different styles and I'm aware that in some districts there are real limitations, burdens, problems that cannot be easily solved or lifted. However, I wonder whether there is more room for play and celebration in every classroom. You never know what a fellow human being is going through. We, as teachers, have the privilege and opportunity to be a bright spot in a student's day. You never know who needed that smile or five minutes to rest. The pressure of our schedules, tasks, and outcome measures can feel overwhelming but at the end of the day we create a physical and emotional space for our students—we are their home away from home and in many ways, it feels like each class becomes a sort of family. We hold a very special place in the hearts and minds of our young students. This special place kind of explains why it can be so strange and awkward for our students to see us out of the classroom or "in the wild" as some students put it. We exist for them in this home away from home. Teachers are magical and can shift someone's entire day—I see it all the time with my colleagues. We need play, joy, and celebration just as much as our students do. Let us be role models for this and as we do this incredibly important and noble work let us also receive as much as we offer.

Dr. Barrett has a wonderful approach to teaching. She reminds us that by modeling self-care, we do more than take care of ourselves; we demonstrate to students and colleagues alike what it looks like to live and work sustainably. In an educational environment that often glorifies overextension and burnout, showing that it's okay to set boundaries, take breaks, and care for oneself is a radical, yet necessary act. It teaches resilience, emotional intelligence, and long-term thinking.

So, How Do We *Model* Self-care Effectively for Our Students?

First, we talk about it openly. We normalize discussions around stress, rest, and the strategies we use to maintain our mental and physical health. When students see that even their teachers—a symbol of discipline and structure—prioritize these things, it validates their own experiences and encourages them to do the same.

We also lead by example by respecting our own limits and encouraging students to do the same. We take time off when needed and speak positively about seeking support. Additionally, we integrate mindfulness, reflection, and balance into our classroom routines. Ultimately, modeling self-care is one of the most meaningful lessons we can teach. It shows students that success doesn't have to come at the expense of well-being—and that thriving is not just possible but the goal.

Burnout often leaves people feeling isolated, even in the middle of a bustling school filled with colleagues and students. Many of us long to be seen, heard, and validated—just as our students do. As educators, we dedicate ourselves to creating safe, supportive environments for our students, but we must also extend that same compassion to ourselves and our colleagues. Supporting one another through active listening, encouragement, and shared experiences is a powerful step toward healing. While we cannot change others, we *can* create a culture where people feel valued and acknowledged. When we uplift those around us, we strengthen ourselves in the process.

Burnout doesn't have to be the end of the road. In fact, it can be a turning point—a signal that something needs to shift, not a sign of failure. With the right mindset, intentional choices, and the support of a caring community, burnout can lead to a renewed, purpose-driven approach to both teaching and life.

The exhaustion can fade. The spark can return. And in its place, you can build a more sustainable, fulfilling way of living and teaching—one rooted in clarity, self-compassion, and alignment with what truly matters to you.

It's not just about surviving the hard seasons—it's about emerging from them with a stronger sense of self and a clearer vision for the future. A life where *you* get to decide who you are, what you value, and how you want to show up in the world.

So, how do you want to show up for your students?

30 A Whole New Approach to Teaching and Learning?

Dr. Andres Paz and Dr. Alfonso Paz have a wonderful approach to education with a powerful, human-first approach: **mental wellness before learning**. Their company, Vibix Learning, focuses on helping students and teachers manage their health before the teaching and learning begins. Dr. Alfonso Paz believes, "Unregulated students cannot learn from unregulated teachers."[1]

For Dr. Andres Paz, years in education taught him that sustainable teaching begins with self-awareness and personal well-being. By intentionally prioritizing his own mental health, he's shifted from reacting to stress to preparing for it—modeling the kind of balance and resilience that empowers both educators and students. His journey shows that when we care for ourselves first, we show up more present, connected, and effective in the classroom.

Dr. Alfonso Paz brings a systems lens to this same belief. He sees wellness not as a luxury but as a prerequisite for meaningful learning—especially in communities where support is limited. His focus is on building environments that embed care into the everyday fabric of schools, where students and educators alike are equipped with tools to manage stress, build awareness, and grow from a place of safety and support.

Together, Andres and Alfonso are shaping a new educational culture—one that values people over performance, and wellness as the foundation, not the afterthought. In this model, learning isn't just academic—it's personal, intentional, and deeply human.

The best advice they can give teachers at any phase of their career is to be self-aware and take a minute when they need to. This seems simple, but it can be a game changer. The notion of pausing, even for just a minute, might feel unconventional or even taboo in today's fast-paced world—but it can be incredibly beneficial. Taking a moment to breathe, reflect, or simply reset can make all the difference in how we show up for ourselves and others.

How do you take a moment? Well, the first thing you do is give yourself permission. You don't need to feel guilty or hide the fact that you need a moment before you begin teaching. Once you are comfortable with your decision, take a walk, get a cup of coffee, spend some time outside, do what helps you relax and reset. Do what fills your bucket so you can be present for your students.

As educators, we're constantly attuned to our students' needs. We notice when they're overwhelmed, distracted, or emotionally taxed—and we respond with empathy. We offer them a moment to pause, to breathe, to gather themselves. We even teach them how to recognize those moments for themselves, fostering self-awareness and emotional intelligence.

But how often do we truly extend that same care to ourselves—or to our fellow educators?

We're quick to notice when a student needs support, but are we as attentive when a colleague is struggling? Have you ever seen a fellow teacher on the verge of burnout, overwhelmed, or emotionally drained? Did you pause to check in? To offer them a chance to step away, even briefly, and take a breath?

The truth is, we all need those moments. And until we build systems and habits that make space for them, we may not always recognize when we—or the people around us—need help.

Being intentional about planning for these pauses, both for yourself and for your team, isn't a luxury; it's a necessity. Creating a culture of care starts with small actions: noticing, offering, and supporting one another in taking that moment to reset.

Because when teachers take care of each other, everyone benefits—including the students we're here to serve.

It's time to shift our mindset. Just as we prioritize the well-being of our students, we must learn to prioritize our own. Supporting one another, recognizing when *we* need a moment, and granting ourselves the same grace we offer our students isn't indulgent—it's essential. The more we model self-care and mutual support, the more sustainable and compassionate our schools become. And when we care for ourselves and each other, learning doesn't just happen—it thrives.

31 *What Can You Do with Your Summer Vacation to Reduce the Symptoms of Burnout?*

As teachers, we are fortunate to have more time off than most other professions. This break is not just a luxury—it's a necessity. The intensity of the school year takes a toll, and summer provides a crucial opportunity to reset, recharge, and rediscover the joy in both teaching and life. However, simply doing nothing will help only to a certain extent. To truly combat burnout, we must be intentional about how we use this time.

So, how can you make the most of summer to support your well-being? The answer lies in identifying what you *truly* need.

Do you need a full break? Many teachers reach the summer months utterly drained. The demands of the school year—constantly following a schedule, managing classroom dynamics, and putting students' needs before their own—leave little room for personal restoration. If this resonates with you, allow yourself a complete break.

Give yourself permission to step out of the professional mindset. Sleep in. Read a novel that has nothing to do with pedagogy. Take spontaneous day trips. Allow yourself to simply *be*, free from rigid plans and daily agendas. Let your mind and body decompress before even beginning to think about school again. Taking the entire summer off isn't just okay—it's a powerful step toward becoming a more energized, present, and effective teacher. There's no guilt in rest; regeneration is essential.

You need to reclaim what teaching takes away from you. Consider what teaching doesn't allow you to do during the school year. Now is the time to reclaim those moments. Is it the freedom to go for a run in the middle of the day? The ability to travel without worrying about grading deadlines? The chance to immerse yourself in a hobby that got pushed aside.

For some, this might mean embracing a creative pursuit—painting, writing, or learning an instrument. For others, it's about physical well-being—developing a consistent workout routine, improving nutrition, or prioritizing rest. Whatever it is, give yourself the space to do it.

Summertime might be the time you rebuild relationships. The demands of teaching often mean sacrificing time with loved ones. Which relationships have taken a backseat during the school year? Who have you missed? Use this time to reconnect with family and friends over coffee, at the dog park, or while sharing a meal. These relationships are vital not only for personal happiness but also for maintaining perspective beyond the world of education.

When you can find a moment, and you are willing to think about school, focus on your biggest challenges from the last school year. What are you *most relieved* to leave behind during summer break? Is it waking up at dawn? Attending endless faculty meetings? Planning differentiated lessons for a packed classroom? Your answer can be revealing. If there's a specific aspect of teaching that drains your energy, acknowledge it. This awareness can help you strategize ways to mitigate its impact in the upcoming school year.

If you want to improve your teaching skills, summer is a great time to grow without pressure. Once you've had time to rest, you might find yourself naturally drawn to professional growth—on *your own* terms. Is there something you wanted to improve upon but never had time for? Maybe it's refining a particular teaching strategy, learning how to better support students with special needs, or exploring artificial intelligence to help students use this tool for learning and avoid plagiarism.

Professional development doesn't have to be dry or mandatory. Get creative. If you teach Geometry, consider taking an art class to improve your ability to illustrate diagrams and concepts. If you're a history teacher, indulge in a deep dive into a historical period you love. The goal is to engage in learning that excites and energizes you—not drains you further.

Before the summer ends, take a moment to reflect. How do you want to show up for your students next year? Visualize the teacher you want to be and consider your needs as well as your students. What small, meaningful changes can you make that will bring more joy into your classroom? Maybe it's incorporating music into your lessons, creating a friendly classroom competition, or establishing new ways to engage students.

Do you need to work in the summer? For some, summer employment is necessary for financial stability or is an opportunity to explore another passion. If you *must* work, consider whether the job contributes to your overall well-being. Does it energize you or exhaust you further? If it drains you, ask yourself whether you have the option to scale back. If you don't *need* to work, allow yourself to enjoy a true break without guilt.

You can use the summer to intentionally prioritize self-care. It's the perfect time to reset and build habits that support your long-term well-being. Reflect on what nourishes your body, mind, and spirit. Consider these questions:

- How can you improve your sleep and feel more rested?
- How can you move your body in ways that bring you joy?
- How can you spend more time outside and connect with nature?
- How can you explore or rediscover a passion or hobby?
- How can you nurture and strengthen your sense of community?
- How can you reduce stress and protect your peace?
- How can you nourish yourself through food, rest, and creativity?
- How can you unplug from work and reconnect with yourself and others?
- How can you build daily rituals that make you feel grounded and whole?

We often think self-care must be intense—major fitness overhauls, strict routines—but the real key is **consistency**. Small, sustainable changes make the biggest impact. If you can establish these habits now, they'll be easier to maintain when the school year begins.

The school year will come again, bringing challenges and rewards. But for now, summer is yours. Treat it as the gift it is. Use it to rest, reconnect, and rediscover yourself—not just as a teacher, but as a person. Be intentional about your summer plans. You have earned this. Enjoy the time and take care of yourself.

32 *What Do You Collect?*

What do you collect? Baseball cards? Fancy watches? Stones that look like hearts? People collect all kinds of things—for fun, for beauty, for nostalgia. But have you ever thought about collecting something that can actually help you navigate burnout?

Here's a Powerful Idea: Start Collecting Thank You Notes.

Over the course of a year—or a career—you'll receive many notes from students, families, and colleagues. They may be handwritten cards, quick texts, or emails expressing appreciation for something you did. Don't toss them. Don't let them get buried in an inbox or forgotten drawer.

Keep them. Treasure them. Revisit them—especially on the tough days when you feel drained, discouraged, or invisible.

This personal archive of gratitude can serve as a quiet reminder of the impact you've made, the lives you've touched, and the value you bring. In a world where burnout often stems from feeling unseen or unappreciated, thank you notes can be an antidote. They reconnect you to your purpose and your people.

So go ahead—start your collection. Find a special box, a folder, or even a drawer where you can tuck away those thank you notes. These small tokens of appreciation are more than just paper—they're reminders of your impact, your presence, your worth.

Make a date with yourself to revisit them at least once a year. Brew a cup of coffee or tea, settle into a quiet space, and take the time to truly absorb the words. Let the gratitude seep in. Let yourself feel it—fully. Let it remind you of the good you've done, the lives you've touched, and the value you bring, even on the days when you forget.

You might be surprised by how deeply it sustains you. And as your collection grows, something beautiful may happen—you'll find yourself inspired to write more thank you notes of your own. A few sincere words can brighten someone's entire week. Pass it on.

Is there a parent who quietly stepped in to support you and your class? An administrator who went the extra mile? A student who's always first to lend a hand? Take a moment to let them know their efforts haven't gone unnoticed. A few sincere words can leave a lasting impact—just as theirs have on you. Never underestimate the power of gratitude. When we give it freely and receive it openly, we build something enduring: connection, purpose, and hope. And when we have those, burnout begins to lose its grip.

Teaching's Parting Gift

Teaching bestows countless gifts upon us. We are honored to serve our students, to delve into our passions, and to savor the long, restorative summers. We lead lives rich in learning and experience the joy of watching young people take risks and grow right in front of our eyes. Yet, for me, the most profound gift has been the assurance that tomorrow brings a fresh start.

If my lesson falls flat, tomorrow is another day. If I lose my patience, tomorrow is another day. If I don't see a child in need, tomorrow is another day.

I think Ralph Waldo Emerson said it best:

> "Finish each day and
> be done with it. You
> have done what you
> could. Some blunders
> and absurdities no
> doubt have crept in;
> forget them as soon
> as you can. Tomorrow
> is a new day. You shall
> begin it serenely and
> with too high a spirit
> to be encumbered with
> your old nonsense."

~Ralph Waldo Emerson~

My prayer for you is that after reading this book, you will start tomorrow with "too high a spirit to be encumbered with your old nonsense." I wish you all the best and please let me know how you are doing. My email is kmcdowell256@gmail.com.

Enjoy and happy teaching!

Notes

Chapter 1

1 LAUSD. Accessed May 23, 2025. https://www.lausd.org/cms/lib/CA01000043/Centricity/domain/625/pdfs/social%20awareness/Article-Power%20of%20Encouragement.pdf.

2 The Educator. "Survey Reveals the Lasting Impact of Teachers." The Educator K/12, March 3, 2024. https://www.theeducatoronline.com/k12/news/survey-reveals-the-lasting-impact-of-teachers/284213.

3 Educator, "Survey Reveals the Lasting Impact of Teachers."

4 Educator, "Survey Reveals the Lasting Impact of Teachers."

Chapter 2

1 Lin, Luona, Kim Parker, and Juliana Menasce Horowitz. "1. Teachers' Job Satisfaction." Pew Research Center, April 4, 2024. https://www.pewresearch.org/social-trends/2024/04/04/teachers-job-satisfaction/.

2 "Burn-out an 'Occupational Phenomenon': International Classification of Diseases." World Health Organization. Accessed June 10, 2025. https://www.who.int/news/item/28-05-2019-burn-out-an-occupational-phenomenon-international-classification-of-diseases.

3 "Where Do You Fall on the Burnout Continuum?" *Psychology Today*. Accessed June 10, 2025. https://www.psychologytoday.com/us/blog/high-octane-women/201205/where-do-you-fall-on-the-burnout-continuum#:~:text=Physical%20and%20mental%20exhaustion%20can,done%20when%20you're%20there.

4 Walker, Tim. "Getting Serious About Teacher Burnout." NEA. Accessed May 23, 2025. https://www.nea.org/nea-today/all-news-articles/getting-serious-about-teacher-burnout.

5 Freudenberger, Herbert J., and Geraldine Richelson. *Burn-out: The High Cost of High Achievement*. Garden City, NY: Anchor Press, 1980.

6 Freudenberger, and Richelson, *Burn-out*.
7 "Projections for Teachers: How Many Are Leaving the Occupation?" U.S. Bureau of Labor Statistics. Accessed May 23, 2025. https://www.bls.gov/careeroutlook/2018/data-on-display/how-many-teachers-are-leaving.htm.
8 Lin, Luona. "What's It Like to Be a Teacher in America Today?" Pew Research Center, April 4, 2024. https://www.pewresearch.org/social-trends/2024/04/04/whats-it-like-to-be-a-teacher-in-america-today/.
9 Lin, "What's It Like to Be a Teacher in America Today?"
10 "Listening to the Educator Experience." Charles Butt Foundation, September 16, 2024. https://charlesbuttfdn.org/what-were-learning/2023txteacherpoll/.

Chapter 3

1 "Teacher Turnover: Why It Matters and What We Can Do about It." Learning Policy Institute, September 25, 2023. https://learningpolicyinstitute.org/product/teacher-turnover-report.
2 US Department of Education. Accessed May 27, 2025. https://ed.gov/news/press-releases/monthly/202210.
3 "Home." Grand Canyon University. Accessed May 27, 2025. https://www.gcu.edu/blog/teaching-school-administration.
4 Guidara, Will. *Unreasonable Hospitality: The Remarkable Power of Giving People More than They Expect*. London: Ebury Edge, 2024.

Chapter 4

1 Ginott, Haim. *Between Parent and Child: The Bestselling Classic That Revolutionized Parent-child Communication*. Revised and updated. New York: Three Rivers Press, 2003.

Chapter 5

1 Dawson, Ben. "Remembering Jaime Escalante." Children's Defense Fund, August 30, 2023. https://www.childrensdefense.org/remembering-jaime-escalante/#:~:text=His%20simple%20formula%20for%20student,the%20hardworking%20and%20committed%20teacher.
2 About Dr. Maria Montessori | The American Montessori Society. Accessed May 27, 2025. https://amshq.org/about-us/history-of-ams/about-dr-maria-montessori/.
3 "Official Website of Bill Nye the Science Guy." Bill Nye. Accessed May 27, 2025. https://www.billnye.com/.

Part 2

1 "Winnie the Pooh & Pals: Official Disney Site." Winnie the Pooh. Accessed May 27, 2025. https://winniethepooh.disney.com/.
2 Manson, Mark. *The Subtle Art of Not Giving a F*ck*. London: Harper & Row, 2019.

Chapter 7

1 "BBC World Service | Learning English | Moving Words." BBC News. Accessed June 10, 2025.
2 Newman, Kira M. "Thinking about Reaching Out to Someone? Science Says Do It." *Greater Good Magazine*, n.d. https://greatergood.berkeley.edu/article/item/thinking_about_reaching_out_to_someone_science_says_do_it#:~:text=Science%20Says%20Do%20It,even%20nicer%20than%20we%20expect.&text=In%20the%20space%20between%20strangers,for%20happiness%20and%20deeper%20relationships.
3 Newman, "Thinking about Reaching Out to Someone? Science Says Do It."

Chapter 8

1 YouTube. Accessed June 10, 2025. https://www.youtube.com/watch?v=gzfhPB_NtVc.
2 Kahneman, Daniel. *Thinking fast and slow*. New York: Farrar, Straus and Giroux, 2011.
3 YouTube. Accessed June 10, 2025. https://www.youtube.com/watch?v=gzfhPB_NtVc.
4 YouTube. Accessed June 10, 2025. https://www.youtube.com/watch?v=gzfhPB_NtVc.

Chapter 9

1 Engelbrecht-Aldworth, Erika. "The Power of Gratitude: Enhancing Teacher and Learner Well-being." LinkedIn, September 7, 2024. https://www.linkedin.com/pulse/power-gratitude-enhancing-teacher-learner-well-being-erika-lzf8f#:~:text=The%20Benefits%20of%20a%20Gratitude,and%20effectiveness%20in%20the%20classroom.
2 "How Gratitude Impacts Your Brain and Behavior." Strobel Education, April 4, 2024. https://strobeleducation.com/blog/how-gratitude-impacts-your-brain/#:~:text=Simple%20acts%2C%20like%20acknowledging%20students,and%20encourage%20a%20growth%20mindset.
3 Rowell, Lainie. *Evolving with Gratitude: Small Practices in Learning Communities That Make a Big Difference with Kids, Peers, and the World*. San Diego, CA: IMpress, 2022.
4 Rowell, *Evolving with Gratitude*.

5 Rowell, *Evolving with Gratitude.*
6 Rowell, *Evolving with Gratitude.*

Chapter 10

1 Perry, Ginger. Lecture. *Chapel Talk*. Presented at the Brooks Chapel, May 2023.

Chapter 11

1 Nouwen, Henri J. M. *You Are the Beloved: Daily Meditations for Spiritual Living.* Convergent Books.

Chapter 15

1 Biesenbach, Rob. *Unleash the Power of Storytelling: Win Hearts, Change Minds, Get Results*. Evanston, IL: Eastlawn Media, 2018.
2 Biesenbach, *Unleash the Power of Storytelling.*
3 Biesenbach, *Unleash the Power of Storytelling.*

Chapter 21

1 "Our Epidemic of Loneliness and Isolation." Accessed June 12, 2025. https://www.hhs.gov/sites/default/files/surgeon-general-social-connection-advisory.pdf.
2 "Our Epidemic of Loneliness and Isolation."

Chapter 23

1 Brooks, David. *How to Know a Person: The Art of Seeing Others Deeply and Being Deeply Seen*. New York: Random House, 2023.
2 Brooks, *How to Know a Person.*

Chapter 27

1 "Every Educator Needs to Know How the Brain Learns." Accessed June 12, 2025. https://www.ascd.org/el/articles/every-educator-needs-to-know-how-the-brain-learns.

2 "Every Educator Needs to Know How the Brain Learns."

Chapter 30

1 Dr. Andrés Paz, Chief Research Officer, VIBIX Learning, Ph.D. Experimental Psychology and Alfonso Paz, CEO, Vibix Learning, apaz@vibixlearning.com, 310-386-2920.

www.ingramcontent.com/pod-product-compliance
Ingram Content Group UK Ltd.
Pitfield, Milton Keynes, MK11 3LW, UK
UKHW020237160926
475610UK00001B/21

9 798765 188958